I0144962

DON'T EVEN THINK ABOUT RIPPING ME OFF

A step-by-step guide on how to
hire, work with and pay your contractor

by PHAE MOORE

Don't Even Think About Ripping Me Off!

Copyright © 2014 by Phae Moore

All rights reserved. No part of this book may be reproduced or transmitted in any form or by any means without written permission of the author.

ISBN   978-0-9897891-0-3

Acknowledgements

There are too many people to name who have been advisors, mentors, counselors, volunteers, helpers and constructive criticizers. You all know who you are and I thank you for helping to make NCPHIF a success!

Kevin Veler, thank you for lending your extensive expertise in construction law to our organization since the day we opened our doors.

To my daughter, Brittany Phae Moore, thank you for your brilliance.

And to all those who have been scammed by home repair contractors, rest assured, I will continue to work hard to prevent it from happening to anyone else. I hope to make you proud.

Table of Contents

Table of Checklists

INTRODUCTION

NCPHIF

The National Center for the Prevention of Home Improvement Fraud

Meet Who You Could Be

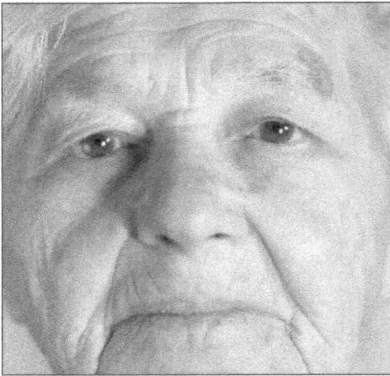

Meet Rose

One day Rose, an elderly widow who lives alone in the house where her children were born, received a knock on the door from a solicitor offering a free roof inspection. Because of recent hail storms in the area, Rose had no reason to be suspicious. Because she can't check the roof herself, Rose gave the man permission to do so. The solicitor went up on the roof, punched holes into some shingles, and informed Rose she needed a new roof. Unsure of what to do, Rose signed a contract for $15,000 and wrote the man a deposit check for $5,000. He promised to be back to complete the work in one week. Many weeks later, there is no contractor, no roof repair, and $5,000 less in Rose's savings account. Distraught, humiliated, and afraid her children will think she can no longer manager her life or finances, Rose does nothing. Meanwhile the solicitor has moved on to the next person who won't see this scam coming.

Meet the Wilson Family

After a tornado hits their community, the Wilson family home suffers extensive damage. Luckily, the Wilsons have insurance to cover most of the damage to the house. Vulnerable and wanting to get back into their home as soon as possible, they endorse a $60,000 insurance check over to a contractor who was on the scene the day after the tornado hit. They move in with friends and wait for the repairs to be made. A week later, they call the contractor to find out when the repairs will start only to find the number has been disconnected. Thinking it must be a mistake, they get on the internet to check out the website address from the contractor's card. It doesn't exist. Desperate, they call the Better Business Bureau, the Secretary of State, and anyone else they think might be able to help them. They are informed that they can file a complaint, but the odds of catching the contractor and getting their money back are slim to none. Victimized twice, the Wilsons are left with an uninhabitable home and no money to repair it. Feeling defeated, they walk away from their home of 14 years and suffer foreclosure. Meanwhile, the contractor is at the next disaster area preying on another vulnerable family ready to take his bait.

Meet Mr. Jones

Mr. Jones is a retired executive from one of Fortune 500's best known international companies. With time on his hands, and a nice retirement account, he decides to finally re-landscape his backyard and add a pool for his grandchildren to enjoy. He finds a listing through a contractor referral service, meets with the contractor to discuss the project, and signs the contract to get the job started. Being a savvy businessman, he pays no deposit or money upfront. When the pool is installed and the landscaping is finished, Mr. Jones writes the contractor a check for $30,000. He is happy with a job well done. Six months later, Mr. Jones finds a lien on his property by a supplier in the amount of $12,000. He finds out that the contractor has gone out of business, owes all his suppliers, and has left Mr. Jones with a liability that could have been avoided. Mr. Jones can sue the contractor, but ultimately he knows it will be valuable time lost, legal fees paid, and little chance of getting any money back.

These are just a few examples of the everyday stories of home repair contractor fraud.

You tell yourself.....that won't happen to me. Or you ask yourself.......could this happen to me?

Yes it can. Yes it absolutely can.

You Are Not Alone!

This book is written to educate you on how to protect yourself from home repair contractor fraud and scams. It is intended to provide a workbook to help you manage a 'fraud free' project. However, the most important thing we want you to know is that you are not alone! If you have any questions, contact us at **www.PreventContractorFraud. org** regardless of where you are in your project or how small you think your question may be.

If there is something in this book that you do not understand or you would like more information on, you can contact us at **www. PreventContractorFraud.org**. We are always available to help you with questions, concerns or comments. You are not alone!

Six Things You Need to Know

Here is some required information we want you to know:

1. All information contained in this book is for informational purposes only and should in no way be considered legal advice. The general information contained herein may not be suitable for every situation. State laws vary, so we highly recommend you

contact a licensed legal professional in your state for any professional or legal advice regarding your home repair project. In fact, throughout this book, we <u>constantly</u> remind you of how important it is to seek the advice of a licensed legal professional in your state before you sign any documentation or enter into any agreements with home repair contractors.

2. Not all contractors are bad! There are millions of professional, honest and reputable contractors all over the world and we applaud them. When we refer to the term *"contractor"* (*depending on the context of the sentence*) it may or may not indicate a *"dishonest"* contractor. It is used to imply a "noun" and is not, in any way, an indication that any contractor in that particular instance is honest or dishonest.

3. From our extensive work nationwide, we have compiled information in this book from all over the country. Some states license certain contractors; other states may not. Some information in this book may not apply to every situation or in every jurisdiction or state. Nonetheless, we bring it to your attention so you can ask the right questions specific to where you live. And remember, you can contact us at **www.PreventContractorFraud.org** for assistance.

4. We are not telling you everything. But we sure are telling you a lot! The contents of this book should give you enough information to help protect you from home repair/rebuild/remodel contractor fraud and scams. It should also help cut down on any miscommunication between you and a legitimate contractor. We would be honored if you would contact us (**www.PreventContractorFraud. org**) with any new information you believe other homeowners should know. We will include those tips in our next edition.

5. You may find that we repeat information throughout the book. We do this because a reader may just go to a specific chapter and miss a lot of important information. However, we encourage everyone to take the time to read the entire book so they don't miss any valuable information.

6. Many of the documents we discuss in this book vary from state to state. Therefore, we did not include pictures of them. If you would like a sample of any of the documents we refer to in this book specific to your state, you can easily find them on the Internet or you can contact us at **www.PreventContractorFraud.org**.

The Two Most Popular Lessons!

1. Even though researching contractors and learning how to manage your project seems like a lot of work in the beginning, it is better to do your homework <u>before</u> you hire anyone. Being safe rather than sorry is old advice, but excellent advice.

2. Never feel rushed. Many homeowners who were scammed say they were in a hurry to get the job over with so they could get back to normal. Yet, they are still going through a long nightmare with their contractors, 1 or 2 years after they hired them. So much for rushing.

Terms

Just a few:

Building Department refers to the local building department. They are the government agency in place to regulate safety in the construction industry.

Contractor, Service Provider or **Vendor** refers to any contractor (*depending on the context of the sentence, it may or may not indicate a "dishonest" contractor*). We want to emphasize that not all contractors are dishonest. Different types of contractors include general or prime contractors, plumbers, electricians, inspectors, engineers, architects, roofers, landscapers, framers, arborists, tile installers, remodelers, homebuilders, developers, storm restoration contractors, public adjusters, carpenters, painters, flooring specialists, debris removers, carpet installers, handymen, bricklayers, window washers, insulators, surveyors, etc.

He/His when referring to contractors, is used to represent any contractor(s), regardless of gender (*for reference only*).

Home Repair refers to any construction, including demolition, installation, renovation, improvements, repairs, remodels, rebuilds, and new construction.

Homeowner refers to any homeowner, future homeowner or small business.

NCPHIF refers to the National Center for the Prevention of Home Improvement Fraud, a national 501(c)(3) not-for-profit whose mission is to educate individuals and communities on how to protect themselves from becoming victims of home repair contractor fraud and scams.

Subcontractor refers to any contractors who are hired by a general contractor or by you, to do a specific job, such as an electrician or plumber.

Supplier refers to any retailer/wholesaler who is supplying any materials, equipment, supplies, etc.

About NCPHIF

The National Center for the Prevention of Home Improvement Fraud (NCPHIF) is a 501c3 nonprofit organization created to educate consumers with "Best Practices" when hiring a contractor to work on their homes or small businesses. Our goal is to provide every community with valuable information and assistance to help keep contractor fraud from happening at all.

NCPHIF does not recommend or endorse any contractor. We provide an unbiased (safe) place for homeowners to go with their questions and concerns regarding home repair projects, hiring contractors, and avoiding home repair fraud. Through NCPHIF, consumers learn how to avoid being victims of outright theft, large upfront deposits, fraudulent insurance claims, illegal contracts, shoddy construction, and liens on the property they have worked so hard to acquire.

Since 2009, we have been educating consumers on the do's and don'ts when dealing with contractors. Our *SmartPower* workshops *"Protecting Yourself from Home Repair Contractor Fraud and Scams"* are well received all over the country, from large cities to small towns.

In disaster areas, NCPHIF sets up its *Home Repair Fraud Prevention Kiosk* to coach disaster victims, one-on-one, on how to navigate their individual rebuild projects. Disaster victims just want to rebuild/repair and get back to normal as quickly as possible. Shady contractors know this and prey on them, making them victims, twice.

NCPHIF has helped hundreds of thousands of consumers and has made its mark as the go-to organization for help when dealing with home repair contractors. Many elected officials, governmental agencies, law enforcement groups, corporate executives, community leaders, neighborhood associations, small businesses and individual homeowners speak highly of the work that NCPHIF has done in their communities.

NCPHIF is committed to helping everyone avoid home repair fraud. The benefits of our work are:

- Homeowners can feel more confident and knowledgeable when overseeing their home repair/rebuild/remodel projects;

- Ethical contractors can focus on providing quality service at reasonable rates while continuing to serve their customers and grow their businesses;

- Insurance companies can better manage their rates with the reduction of fraudulent claims;

- Lenders will have fewer foreclosures as informed homeowners avert the financial problems commonly brought on by contractor fraud;

- Government offices, law enforcement agencies, and businesses can spend less time and money pursuing dishonest contractors as fraud complaints decline.

Our Mission

NCPHIF's long-term mission is to make every city and town in the United States a "*fraud free*" zone. We believe by educating homeowners on fraud prevention, we will help make the process easier and ensure the delivery of competent services to homeowners, as well as boot shady contractors out of the construction industry. This knowledge helps homeowners receive the best value from honest contractors while ensuring these honest professionals are treated fairly and objectively by the homeowners they serve.

Our Founder

NCPHIF was founded by its Executive Director, Phae Moore, a home repair fraud prevention expert, after witnessing first-hand her grandmother being financially and emotionally victimized by a dishonest contractor. *"I absolutely remember the pain in her face,"* Phae says. *"That will be with me always."* Phae realized that, like her grandmother, many homeowners are not equipped with the information and resources to avoid becoming victims of home repair fraud. She has made it her personal goal, and the mission of NCPHIF, to give potential victims the necessary tools to avoid similar situations. Phae believes that now more than ever, the need for NCPHIF's services is not only critical, it is urgent.

Phae continues to bring awareness to this problem. *"If I don't work hard every day to reach and teach every community how to protect themselves, if I don't knock on every door for the support NCPHIF needs to help protect those who are most vulnerable to contractor scams in this country, then I am doing them all a disservice,"* she says.

CHAPTER 1

Shady Contractors and Typical Victims

What Does a "Shady" Contractor Look Like?

Many people expect shady contractors to look or act like "*bad guys*". You might expect a dishonest contractor to have on dirty clothes and smell like he has been drinking alcohol all day. Or you might expect a scam artist to have a "*slick*" look. Truth is, they come in all shapes, sizes, colors, and classes. He certainly is not wearing a tee-shirt that says "*I'm Dishonest.*" But we can tell you that they are pros at gaining your confidence and experts at coming across as charming, persuasive, friendly and helpful. People who think they are a good judge of character and think they can spot a con artist are very vulnerable. Con artists are experts at dealing with those who think they cannot be victimized.

Leaving the Door Open for Shady Contractors

Year after year, communities nationwide fall victim to unscrupulous agents posing as skilled, legitimate, licensed and bonded home repair contractors. Every homeowner is a potential victim.

Sadly, these dishonest individuals are experienced and well versed in many tactics and easily prey on consumers' lack of knowledge.

There is not enough protection for homeowners when it comes to shady contractors. There are too few laws to regulate and punish offenders. Some laws have been passed recently; however, they are not really enforced as much as we would like to see. This leaves the door wide open for fraud and scams. More can and should certainly be done.

Accurate data on the extent of contractor fraud is difficult to obtain. Many victims fail to report cases out of embarrassment or lack of awareness that they have, in fact, been victimized.

Because of their financial or educational status, many do not consider themselves possible targets. Others are unsure of how to report contractor fraud or are confused about what government agency actually has the responsibility and authority to investigate and prosecute scammers. Many are discouraged after completing mounds of complaint forms only to be told there is nothing the agency can do for them. Most agencies don't have the resources to battle this problem. And dishonest contractors can change their names, contact information, and location to defraud new, unsuspecting homeowners.

Trade associations in the construction industry do have complaint procedures, but unfortunately, most often they lack the power to push contractors to correct problems.

For law enforcement agencies, prosecuting consumer fraud is tough because more often than not, homeowners do not report that they have been scammed. And when they do, local police may not have enough resources. In many cases, the matter is considered civil, not criminal. As a result, many victims feel there is no need in taking the time to report it or fill out lengthy paperwork.

Impact of Dealing with a Shady Contractor

The homeowner is the immediate loser. Not only have they lost their money and time, but their sense of security and sometimes dignity as well. The anger and embarrassment of being taken advantage of can lead to marital problems, family arguments and even depression. As fraud victims often experience stress-related complications, the long-term effects can be immeasurable.

After dealing with a dishonest contractor, correcting their shoddy work can often exceed the cost of the original repair. It can take twice the effort, time and money to be redone correctly by a legitimate contractor. A homeowner may not be able to replace money lost. Depressed, they may feel they have no choice but to walk away and abandon the property, resulting in foreclosure by the lender. Foreclosed and abandoned properties lead to lowered property values in neighborhoods. Empty structures become havens for squatters, criminal activity and unsafe conditions in the community. Everyone loses when homeowners are scammed.

Other losers in contractor fraud are lenders who need to protect their investment in the properties they finance and government agencies who must respond to the fraud once it has happened. Also, the insurance industry has a large fraud problem which impacts the premium every homeowner pays, not just those who have repairs. Finally, legitimate contractors suffer as they must now focus more on proving their reputation than just making an honest living.

Some Interesting Facts

According to the Joint Center for Housing Studies of Harvard University, every year since 2007 more than $270 billion is spent on home remodel/repair projects. We believe that more than 5 percent of those dollars are lost to dishonest contractors and shoddy construction. That's over $13.5 billion annually!

Hurricane Katrina is probably one of the greatest examples of the widespread dangers of fraud throughout the nation's multi-billion-dollar-a-year construction industry. After the storm, predators posing as contractors took advantage of thousands of vulnerable, grief stricken homeowners. NCPHIF estimates that unreported fraud and scams could easily triple or quadruple any amount reported.

Outside of disaster-related rebuilds like Katrina, the economy has a direct impact on the home improvement industry. Homeowners either update their homes because they want a new look or upgrade their homes to compete in a buyer's market. Either way, the opportunity for contractor fraud exists. Everyone wins when consumers have awareness, resources, and education to make good, informed decisions when it comes to hiring a contractor.

At Some Point, You are Going to Have to Hire a Contractor

As a homeowner, dealing with a home repair contractor is pretty much inevitable. At some point, you are going to have to deal with a contractor.

- Sometimes typical home maintenance and repairs require the services of a contractor. You may need a roofer, electrician, painter, plumber, builder, etc.

- Sometimes you just want to improve your home by adding space as your children grow, or because you now dislike something, like your blue bathtub. You may want to redo something you believe will help your home sell quicker—maybe upgrade your kitchen countertops or redesign a bathroom.

- Sometimes circumstances beyond your control force you to hire a construction professional. A tornado rips your house in half or shifts your home off its foundation. Hurricane rains flood your basement. A dead tree crushes your roof and breaks windows. Sparks from a fire at your neighbor's house ignites yours. A pipe bursts. Hail severely damages your roof. The list can go on and on.

How This Book Can Help You Avoid Being Scammed

Time and time again, homeowners who contacted NCPHIF said if they could do things over again, they would have done more research up front. They would have chosen the contractor much more carefully. This book is intended to use the lessons they learned *the hard way* to help you avoid repeating their nightmare and financial hardship. It describes various scams as well as tips on how to avoid them. It's a workbook, giving you a step-by-step guide on how to deal with home repair contractors to help you navigate your way through to a successful project.

The steps laid out in this book may seem time consuming and labor intensive, but skimp now and you will likely spend hours and even more money trying to fix a nightmare down the road. It is so much better to do the work up front so you don't have to deal with the headache of a project gone wrong. Being proactive is critical.

Once the contractor disappears with your money or has performed shoddy construction, more often than not, it is too late to recover your losses. Attempts to seek justice when you've been cheated and deceived can be a long, frustrating and very painful process that involves going from agency to agency looking for justice, only to find none. Getting money back from a scammer, even after receiving a favorable judgment from court, is never guaranteed. You may never see a penny. The contractor may have disappeared and can't be found. He may not have the money to repay you. His business may close its doors or file for bankruptcy. Or he may simply refuse to pay. That's why it is important you educate yourself about contractor fraud and prevention strategies before you hire anyone to take on your home repair project.

The easiest way for a thief to get into your home is to represent himself as a contractor.

Am I a Target?

Dishonest service providers and many hardcore salespeople know who to target when it comes to persuading someone to hire them. Anyone can be a target of a scam or poor workmanship. However, predators typically pursue the most vulnerable consumers. Here are some:

- **Those who feel they cannot be scammed** are one of the largest groups of victims. Several mayors, police chiefs, celebrities, detectives, doctors, wealth managers, lawyers and other non-typical victims have advised us that they were scammed or received shoddy service. They feel as though they should have known better and are embarrassed.

- **Storm and disaster victims** (*hurricanes, tornadoes, fires, floods, etc.*) are in a hurry to rebuild so they can get back to normal. They are considered one of the easiest targets as they are already traumatized, shaken and off-guard. This makes them extremely vulnerable.

- **Senior citizens** are huge targets. They own older homes that may need repairs often. They generally have access to cash from a lifetime of savings or equity in their homes. Some who live alone may feel intimidated by a pushy contractor and agree to a dishonest pitch. Most seniors are very hesitant to report they have been scammed, to avoid being perceived as unable to care for themselves anymore.

- **First time homebuyers** have never dealt with a contractor before and many times have no idea of the process. When they were renting, all they had to do was call the landlord when something needed to be repaired.

- **Low wealth communities** are easy targets of discounts, deals, and insurance fraud, and may feel the need to cut corners to save money. Once they are victimized, these homeowners suffer greatly because more often than not, they cannot replace the lost money or afford to pay someone to repair the shoddy construction. Many times they feel the pressure to walk away and foreclose.

- **Those who speak English as a second language** may not understand the terms of a contract or their legal rights and many times don't report being scammed in an effort to not bring attention to themselves.

- **The physically impaired** may not be able to get into areas, such as on the roof or into the crawl space, to verify they need repairs. Many times they rely on anything the contractor tells them.

- **Homeowners in rural areas** may not have many local reputable contractors to choose from.

- **Women** may not be well versed in construction and/or repair procedures or language.

- **Environmentally Conscious Consumers** are some of the newer targets for scams. Greenwashing is basically green energy fraud.

Greenwashing

"Going green" is now the latest trend for home repair/rebuild/re-model projects and dishonest contractors are looking to cash in. Many salespeople and contractors use words like *energy efficient* or *sustainability* making their sales pitch sound like something you must absolutely purchase. They may have devices that look like they can read your entire electrical system with the press of a button. They promise huge energy savings on your utility bills. Many times, celebrities will be hired to appear in ads to get you to believe in a product. Don't just go by what you hear. Investigate. You should ask questions. Has the product been tested by a reputable company? If so, what company? And if they show you independent studies, testing, certifications, etc., don't believe that information. Many fake certifications have been reported. Be sure to verify any energy efficient product(s) with the manufacturer.

Salespeople may tell you there are rebate programs through the government or your local utility company, if you purchase and install their energy efficient appliances in your home. They may suggest that you can get tax credits, refunds, rebates, etc. They tell you they know the process and can fill out paperwork for you to get refunded by the government or utility company. The only true confirmation of any governmental refund program is by the government itself. The Department of Energy (*energy.gov*) and/or the Environmental Protection Agency (*energystar.gov*) are good places to start asking questions. And you can always contact your local utility company to see if they have any rebate/refund programs (*because sometimes they actually do*). Whatever you do, never rely on what a contractor tells you. Always verify the information.

The "yellow sticker" you see on many appliances is supposed to indicate energy efficiency. With advanced technology, it's easy to recreate this yellow sticker. There are many awesome websites that can give you information on green energy terms, regulations and products. You can do an internet search of the term "going green" and you will find all the information you need.

Simply put, if you own a home or are planning to own a home, you are always a potential victim. To think that you are not may be dangerous. Are you smarter than a dishonest contractor?

CHAPTER 2

CHAPTER 2

Ready to Begin Your Project

First Things First

It is time to begin your project. Every project requires planning. When you do your own planning, it helps you understand what you want or need, how to get it done and what the cost is to do it. This cuts down on the frequent miscommunication between homeowners and contractors, even legitimate ones. Being your own quality control manager is the best way to handle the home repair process. Don't know where to begin? Don't worry. Let's start with the first thing: understanding who is boss!

The Boss!

This is your house, your money, and your project. That makes you the boss. Any contractor you hire works for you. They can advise you (*which is why you are hiring knowledgeable, informed contractors*), but you get to make the final decisions.

Your Project

So you have a new project. The first thing you need to determine is exactly what you need or want to have done. It could be a home improvement project like upgrading, remodeling, or expanding your home. It could be landscaping. On the other hand, your project may be the result of circumstances beyond your control (*damage incurred as a result of a storm, a fire, a tree falling on your home, etc.*). In any situation, there is a lot to think about, plan for and oversee.

Start by creating a file folder to keep all of your paperwork together.

Now, in the checklist below, detail what you want to have done as best you can. Don't worry if it's not perfect, it's a start.

CHECKLIST: What Job Needs to be Done	Write Your Information Here:
Emergency Home Repair: Do you need emergency work after a disaster? Did a tree fall on your home? Is your roof leaking after a hail storm? Did a pipe burst? Is your home flooded? Was there a fire? Etc.	
Non-emergency Home Repair: Do you have a home repair project that is not an emergency? Is your air conditioning not working? Your water pressure is low? You need a crack in the ceiling repaired? Etc.	
Elective Home Improvement/Remodel: Do you want to upgrade a kitchen (*new cabinets, fixtures, countertops*)? Add a new bathroom? Etc.	
Project Schedule: When would you like the project to start? What date would you like to have the job completed by?	

Now that you know exactly what you need or want to have done, you need to know how much money it will cost. Now is the time to determine what your budget is. If your budget is open, still do your research to help you determine, as realistically as possible, what your project will cost. The research will help you decide what your budget should be.

Financial Management

You now have to determine how much money you need and how you are going to get it.

Financing: How are You Going to Pay?

You may already have the money under your mattress or in your bank account to fund the project. You may be waiting for your insurance company to issue funds or you are seeking financing to get the project done. Regardless of where you get your money, there are some things you need to be aware of when dealing with financing and your contractor.

Using a finance company recommended by a contractor can be risky business. Some consumers will not look as carefully into the program because funding is included. NCPHIF would encourage you to keep funding separate from the contractor's work and price because we consider this a conflict of interest. We strongly suggest you consider starting your search for funding with your own bank, credit union, etc.

In the event you decide to use the contractor's funding source, know *before you sign anything* what your interest rate will be. Always look for the APR (Annualized Percentage Rate) and what the monthly cost will be. Make sure there are no penalties for paying the loan off early. If this information is not spelled out or you aren't sure about something, always have a trusted financial advisor or attorney review the paperwork before you sign anything.

Be careful borrowing money from finance companies you have never heard of or which you don't know their reputation. Perform an Internet search on the company and see if there are any complaints. Remember, NCPHIF always suggests starting with your own bank or credit union for funding.

Request that the check from the lender is issued to you, *not the contractor.* Giving the check directly to the contractor is trouble. He may not finish the work or worse, take off with the money. If the check is given to the contractor, YOU may still be responsible to pay back the lender, even if the work was never performed. The lender may not verify that the work is properly done or get involved in any payment disputes.

Sometimes, the lender will be involved with the project. If this is the case, be sure to ask your loan officer how they participate in the process. Do they screen the subcontractors? Do they require invoices for materials before they release any payments? Do they get lien waivers? Do they pay the contractor by percentage of work done? If so, ask them what constitutes *"percentage of work"* in terms of your project. For instance, what exactly is *"25 percent of work"*? Does that mean the floors will be done? Cabinets in? Percentage of work can mean different things to different people. Be sure it is clarified.

Keep a copy of all of the documents and information given to you in your file. If you have a problem later with the lender or contractor, having this information may help identify violations of laws which may give you federal and state rights. Check with a trusted financial and/or legal advisor if you need more information specific to your state and your situation.

NEVER ignore any payments, demands or communications from the lender because you have a dispute with the contractor. If you don't understand what is being demanded from or communicated to you, talk with your legal advisor.

The Budget

Ideally, you would like to know what your budget (*a realistic budget*) is going to be. This may be difficult to determine without researching the many aspects of your project. Maybe you are still waiting for your insurance company to send a claims adjuster to determine how much damage you have and how much they are going to pay to have the work done. Maybe you are applying for a home equity line of credit to upgrade your home and are waiting on a response from the lender. (*In some instances, getting pre-qualified by your lending institution may help you determine what your budget will be.*)

Always put aside an extra 10-20 percent of your project budget for unforeseen but legitimate changes to the original project (*especially if you have an older home*). A price increase is not always a scam. Additional costs may be justifiable if they relate to hidden or structural problems not discovered until after the project is underway. A missing stud, frayed or inadequate wiring, water intrusion or other problems may be hidden until a wall is opened.

In an effort to create a budget, answer as many of the questions on the following worksheet as you can. Then move on. At this stage, you probably don't know how much the labor and materials will cost for your particular job. Don't worry. You can always come back to this section and make edits/additions once you have more information.

Now that you have an idea of what you would like to have done, how much money you need to budget for the job, and when you want the project to be completed, you have a foundation. Do not worry about the exercise appearing imperfect or incomplete. It's a start! Going forward you will be working with the people who have specific and credible knowledge, which you can add to or change on your worksheet later.

✓ **CHECKLIST:** **The Budget**	**Write Your Information Here:**
What is your maximum budget? (This information is for you only. Do not share this information with the contractor.)	
How are you going to pay for the project? Do you already have the cash? Are you going to finance the project? If so, are you getting a loan from YOUR bank or another lending institution? Waiting for your insurance company to issue a check?	
What is the estimated total of your materials? (See CHECKLIST: Wishlist)	
What is your estimated labor cost? (You are not really sure because you don't have estimates/quotes yet, but you will. In the meantime, for a rough estimate, just assume it is 40-50 percent of the cost of materials.)	
Add your estimated materials total and your labor costs. Then add, let's say, 20 percent of that sum for your additional or unexpected costs or overages (especially for older homes).	$_____ estimated materials $_____ estimated labor $_____ estimated overages
Now add the estimated materials, labor and overages. This is your ESTIMATED budget. (This number will probably change after you do your research and get quotes; this just gives you something to start with.)	$_____

Plan Your Project

You already have an idea of the type of project you want to do and roughly how much it will cost. Now, it is time to educate yourself about the requirements to get it done.

Research is Key

The first thing to do is research. You want to gather all the information you can and get answers to all your questions. Your inquiries will help you get a better grasp of what it takes for a contractor to complete your project.

We know you may not be a construction expert, so there is no right or wrong way to research your particular project. The important thing is to educate yourself, up front, by learning as much as you can about what your project entails, so you are well versed on the essential and critical aspects of the job. *"Knowing your stuff"* alerts dishonest contractors that you are not an easy target for rip-offs. You will be proud of what you've learned and how empowered you feel!

Here's another great thing: legitimate contractors will appreciate that you took the time to understand their processes and language.

You can always start by researching the subject on the Internet. Now, don't believe everything you read there, of course, but it's a good place to begin. You will see conflicting information, so pick your sources carefully. National construction trade organizations have some good basic information on their websites, information you may not even realize you needed. Manufacturers have specific information regarding their products on their websites as well.

You can also attend local **DIY (Do It Yourself)** workshops in your area or view home renovation/design shows on TV. Keep in mind, the work looks easy on these shows when done by professionals, where mistakes can be edited out and hours of work are shortened to a few minutes of video. You may not see all of the preparation work or you may have other issues that are not dealt with in the DIY show, but you can learn some things.

Take the time to visit construction retail stores. They are truly a good resource for credible, free information. You'll be able to see, hear, touch and compare materials, get cost information and pick up other clues to getting your project done. You can even tell the retail experts you are not sure what your budget should be and ask how long they think the project should take. In your visit to a construction retailer, research the cost of materials, supplies, and tools while you are there.

Ask them all the questions you want. What's the difference between oak cabinets and maple cabinets? Which toilets save the most water? Which pipes should I use in my bathroom? What is the best flooring for basements? What is the best lumber for a deck? If I sit a hot pot on a marble countertop, will it burn?

When you choose products in the planning stage, be sure to write down any particular brands, sizes, types (*of wood, stone, tile, etc.*), grade, models, exact colors, quality, unit price, serial number, etc. Terms like *high quality fixtures* or *eggshell paint* may mean something different to you than to your contractor. If you don't specify the grade of your supplies/materials, he is free to use the cheapest he can find, and you may end up with substandard products.

Be aware of anything that states *"or equal to"*. Equal might be equal, but it may not be something you personally like or want. Keep in mind there are different standards of items (*examples: low grade, standard, builder's choice, high end/luxury, etc.*). You need to know what the standard is of the materials that will be installed on your project. If the item you choose is out of stock or discontinued, what is your "Plan B"? Don't let a contractor decide for you.

Depending on the size and complexity of your project, you may need to hire a licensed architect, engineer, drafting firm, code certified inspector, qualified designer, or design-build professional to complete a set of plans (*building plans, drawings, blueprints, site plans, etc.*) showing exactly what you want built. For instance, if you want to install a swimming pool, you may need to hire a qualified soil engineer before the pool design and construction is started. The information you gather from these sources will give you very good insight into the makeup of an excellent quote from a contractor. If you need to contact one of these specialists, you should check them out as well.

An architect/engineer can also help you determine what you need to do to get the job started, advise you on required building/construction standards, give you information about permits and local licensing requirements, etc. You can also call your local or national homebuilders association to ask even more questions about how to get your project done, like what kind of plans you will need drawn up, and what type of contractor is qualified to do it.

✓ CHECKLIST: Wishlist	Write Your Information Here:
Detail what you will need to have done to your home (as best you can). For example, installing a new kitchen: 'I will need cabinets, tile flooring, appliances, sink, and countertops. I will also need someone to remove the old appliances and cabinets, flooring and countertop.'	
What type of materials/supplies do you need/want? Example: For a new kitchen, what type of cabinets do you want? Oak? Maple? How many cabinets do you need to purchase? What is the cost of these materials (roughly)? (Use this for your materials/supply estimate in your CHECKLIST: The Budget)	

If possible, sketch your project. (Don't worry if you're not a professional graphic artist. Just do the best you can.)

CHAPTER 3

Insurance Issues You Need to Consider

The information contained in this section is for informational purposes only. Insurance and related law varies significantly by jurisdiction. For professional insurance advice, consult with your personal insurance agent or your attorney.

Risk Management and Insurance – General Considerations

Everyone who begins a significant home repair or remodel project wants to see it through without having anyone injured or property damaged. You would like to be sure you've done everything possible to prevent accidents/damage to your home and its contents. Many manuals have been written about workplace safety. It's not this book's purpose to go into detail on creating and maintaining a safe work environment. After all, much of that responsibility falls on the people doing the work and is not within the control of the homeowner. On the other hand, part of managing risk is making sure the right insurance coverage is in place so that if anything happens, you are properly protected.

Note: Every homeowner should have an inventory of their belongings. If a disaster happens, having a record of all your belongings will come in handy when you have to show your insurance company what you lost. Your insurance company has an inventory checklist. Ask your agent for one.

There are three major areas of insurance regarding your home we want to talk about briefly. These are Property insurance, Casualty insurance and Surety Bond coverage. We'll take a closer look at each of these.

- **Property insurance**, which is typically part of your home-owners insurance, covers your home and contents in case of property damage related to a variety of perils such as fire, windstorms, etc. This is often called *First Party Coverage* as you are the person who has a claim with your own insurance company for a covered loss.

- **Casualty insurance** is also typically a part of your homeowner's policy and is often referred to as *Third Party Insurance* because it protects you from claims made by people against you for injury or damage. This would include a visitor who slips and falls on your property as well as any accidents or injuries that arise out of your alleged negligence. Besides being sure that you have the right coverage, you also need to make sure that your contractors and subcontractors have the right coverage, including workers' compensation.

- Finally, there is **Surety Bond** coverage. Usually, bond coverage applies when a contractor does something, or fails to do something, other than what was promised. While not mandatory, they can be very important levels of protection in the home repair process. Given that, when a contractor says he is "*bonded*" you need to know exactly what that means and whether additional protections are warranted.

Bonds

There are several types of surety bonds used in the construction trades industry. You must understand bonds and what it means when a contractor tells you he is "*licensed and bonded.*" Your question to a contractor who says "*I/we are bonded*" should be "*bonded how?*"

The information provided herein does not include *all* the details regarding bonds. We strongly suggest that you contact your insurance agent or trusted advisor to have them explain bonds to you regarding your specific project. Be sure to ask your insurance agent about the *pros and cons* of any bonds you are considering.

> **Note:** Be sure to know what the time limitations are for filing a claim on a bond. When you file a bond claim, very detailed records of the day-to-day facts surrounding the occurrence are usually required. Make sure you work with a reputable bond company. Bond scams exist too!

Keep in mind the information below is general, as each state may have varying guidelines and regulations for bonds.

Performance Bonds

You may want to have your contractor obtain a **performance bond** especially for big/expensive projects. Generally, performance bonds guarantee the satisfactory completion of a project and may provide protection in the event of a **contractor default** (*a failure of performance*) like skipping out without completing your project. The bonding company usually has the option of hiring another contractor or settling with you for damages. If your project is big or costly, you may want to require your contractor get a performance bond and list you as an **obligee** *(a person to whom another is bound by a contract or legal procedure).*

Often, you the homeowner, may end up paying the bond fee. That is not necessarily a bad thing. Posting a performance bond may be worth your investment if your contractor gets sick, vanishes, dies or otherwise fails to perform the work.

Payment Bonds

Payment bonds guarantee that the homeowner will not have any liens for labor or materials filed against their property. This might be something to consider, especially on larger and more expensive home repair or remodeling projects.

Make sure you have a thorough understanding of the bond, its pros and cons, before you obtain one. Your insurance agent should be able to explain any bond issues you need to understand.

As a side bar, a payment bond's benefit to you is that the bond company will evaluate the contractor's financial standing, which may help prevent you from hiring a contractor on the brink of bankruptcy or financial dissolution.

Here are a few other bonds we want to make you aware of:

Maintenance Bonds

Maintenance bonds guarantee against defective materials or workmanship, but usually only for a limited time.

Code Compliance Bonds

In some jurisdictions, a **code compliance bond** may be required by the city or county to cover the failures of a contractor to comply with building code.

Contractor License Bonds

Contractor license bonds are surety bonds in which the bond company promises that the contractor will comply with state licensing laws for contractors, but they may offer homeowners no real remedy for any problems. If your state law permits (*and not all states do*), there may be a process (*after a hearing and finding by a state board of a violation by the contractor*) that allows the consumer to file a claim against the bondholder. Not all violations may permit recovery by the homeowner. And, you may have to submit considerable documentation/information to plead your case. This is another example of when you should contact your insurance agent or advisor.

Completion Bonds

Completion bonds are distinct from and not the same as performance bonds. Completion bonds are used, more often than not, between landowners or developers and counties or lenders to ensure that a proposed development (*i.e., subdivision*) is completed. Completion bonds aren't typically used in homeowner-contractor agreements.

Your Insurance

Prior to starting ANY construction project, we cannot stress enough the importance of contacting your insurance agent to advise him or her of your project before you begin. Advanced notice to your insurance agent can ensure you have the appropriate insurance coverage. Confirming proper coverage is very, very important, because certain work may not be covered, or there may be limitations on the *value* level of coverage. Are you covered if the value of your home increases because of a project? For example, if you installed a new gourmet kitchen but didn't give notice to your insurance agent, and the house burns down, the money you spent on that new kitchen may not be covered under your current homeowner's policy.

Make sure you keep all your proper documentation as to the quality, cost, etc., of materials on any addition to your home.

We highly suggest you ask your insurance agent to explain what coverage your homeowner's policy actually includes and what other coverage may be available (*sinkholes, earthquakes, etc.*), which can be different depending on where you live. You don't have to purchase any insurance coverage you don't want, but at least know what your options are.

> **A Story:** A homeowner thought he was covered when a sinkhole swallowed up his back yard! Confident his insurance company would pay, he filed a claim without speaking to his insurance agent first. The claim was denied. Had this homeowner spoken with his agent first, he would have discovered he did not have sinkhole coverage before he filed the claim.

One critically important thing to know is whether your policy comprises **actual cash value coverage** or **replacement cost coverage**. In some insurance policies, the settlement procedures are a combination of both. Ask your agent about the cost differential. Have him explain the pros and cons of each. Many homeowners become upset when they discover that their policy does not include replacement cost of their current possessions and only pays the depreciated value. But, in the insurance company's defense, this information is given to you annually.

We encounter many homeowners who are upset with their insurance company for denying all or part of a claim. Many times, homeowners do not understand exactly what their homeowner's insurance policy covers until after a disaster happens. Too often, these denials are the result of misunderstandings or lack of knowledge by homeowners about what their policy covers. As an example, a sudden leak of water from a broken water pipe may be covered (*including replacement of floors*), but a slow drip that causes mold in walls and the floor may not. Both are the results of "water leaks" but coverage differs. Choosing the least expensive coverage or ignoring options may not be a good idea, especially if something goes wrong later. In our work, we find that miscommunication between insurance agents and homeowners is a huge issue! One that we believe can be avoided if you educate yourself on exactly what coverage you do and do not have.

Don't let your contractor interpret your insurance policy language. And never let your contractor try to discourage you from contacting your insurance company. This is a huge red flag. The contractor may tell you that he can "*deal with your insurance company*" on your behalf and get you extra money. NCPHIF strongly discourages you from participating in this process through the contractor or an adjuster *suggested* by the contractor. Often, it is indicative of a scam—an activity by an unlicensed adjuster—and may result in a fraudulent act and a compromise of your claim.

The contractor (*or suggested company or individual*) is not a party to your homeowner's policy, so they have nothing to lose if your insurance company decides to terminate you because of your consent and/or participation in a fraudulent act. And you don't want your insurance company to think for a second that you were a party to any fraudulent activity, especially if you had no idea!

If you have concerns regarding the amount of your claim or about the way the claim is being handled, ask to speak to a manager. If you are still not satisfied, consider consulting with an attorney or a licensed Public Adjuster. Just be sure any independent public adjuster is licensed in your state. Your state's Department of Insurance can assist you with determining this information. Keep in mind that you, the homeowner, pay the public adjuster, so only consider hiring one if you think the settlement increase they can help you get will exceed their fee.

Your public adjuster and your contractor should be two totally different people in order to avoid any conflicts of interest. More often than not, contractors are not licensed public adjusters, so don't let him interpret your insurance policy for you.

> **Note:** Be very careful before signing any agreement with a public adjuster. They typically charge you a percentage of the money you get from your insurance company. See what your insurance company tells you they are going to give you for your repairs. If you are not satisfied with the amount they offer, then you can consider a public adjuster.

> **A Story:** A homeowner signed a contract with a public adjuster before he knew what the insurance company was offering. Days later, he received a $100,000 check from the insurance company. When he told the public adjuster he received the check, the public adjuster sent him a bill for $10,000, even though the public adjuster had done nothing yet.

Flood Insurance

Flood Insurance is now offered through FEMA's National Flood Insurance Program. Just a few inches of water from a flood can cause tens of thousands of dollars in damage. Typically, there's a 30-day waiting period from date of purchase before your flood policy goes into effect. For more information on flood insurance, visit **floodsmart.gov.** Be sure to ask what is and is not covered, especially if you have a basement.

> **Note:** If you live in a flood zone, be sure to ask your flood insurance representative if an **elevation certificate** (*a certificate that states you are in compliance with flood elevation requirements in your area*) is necessary.

> **NCPHIF TIP:** Take the time to have your insurance agent sit down with you and explain what your policy actually covers and what other options you have. Remember, fully understanding what insurance coverage you have is ultimately your responsibility and sometimes, especially after a disaster, it can be devastating to find out you aren't covered for something.

The Contractor's Insurance

Before you hire a contractor, you need to be certain the contractor has appropriate insurance coverage (*general liability, workers' compensation, etc.*). Your insurance agent may help you determine what insurance the contractor should have, if you need help. You don't want something to go wrong, and then find out that your contractor did not have enough insurance to cover your losses.

Be sure to ask your contractor for his insurance card or **Certificate of Insurance** (COI). Any reputable contractor should be willing to ask his insurance company to send you a COI. If he refuses, don't use him. If he gives you a copy of the COI rather than having his insurance company send it to you, then call the insurance company to *verify* that all the information is active and current.

The Contractor's Certificate of Insurance should include, at least, the following:

- Name of the insurance company
- Name of the insured (should be exact name on your contract, etc.)
- Policy number
- Date the certificate was issued
- Effective date of the policy
- Expiration date of the policy
- Aggregate/Per Occurrence Limits

You should also consider asking to be listed on the contractor's insurance policy as an *"additional insured."* He won't be happy about it and it may cost you, but it gives you a great deal more protection.

There are recurring debates regarding exactly what a **contractor's general liability insurance** may cover. If a contractor does NOT install a window correctly and the window leaks, the general liability may cover the damages caused by the leak but not the incorrect installation. These insurance issues are rising in a number of states and cases are being decided. The point is that insurance may not cover a contractor's poor workmanship but may cover some of the results of that workmanship. Therefore, insurance is NOT a replacement for checking out the contractor.

> **Note:** If you plan to act as your own general contractor or builder, make sure you discuss this with your insurance agent first. If you hire other people to do any of the work, your insurance policy may not cover all damages or injuries suffered on your property during the project. If an injured worker is deemed to be your employee and you do not have workers' compensation insurance, you

may be subject to the full costs of the injuries and lost wages, plus penalties. Be sure you understand what your individual policy covers and whether other/special coverage is needed.

✓ CHECKLIST: Insurance Coverage	Check Off
Have you contacted your insurance agent to inform them of your home repair needs or home improvement plans and to confirm that you are covered for appropriate risks during that repair or improvement?	
Has your insurance agent explained other coverage available to you which you do not currently have? (*Remember, you don't have to purchase additional types of coverage, but at least know what your options are.*)	
Do you have an inventory of all your belongings?	
Has your insurance agent confirmed that your homeowner's policy provides the appropriate coverage during and after your project?	
Are there any gaps in coverage between your policy and the contractor's policy?	
Should you consider a surety bond for your project?	
Do you know what happens in the event of theft of your belongings or theft of materials and products from your property during the project?	

CHAPTER 4

Selecting the Contractor

The Contractor

Now that you know what your project is, determined your budget, completed your research, understand proper insurance coverage and the critical aspects of your project, it is time to find a contractor to do the work.

There are many different types of contractors: general contractors, plumbers, electricians, inspectors, engineers, architects, roofers, landscapers, framers, arborists, tile installers, remodelers, home-builders, developers, storm restoration contractors, public adjusters, carpenters, painters, flooring specialists, debris removers, carpet installers, handymen, bricklayers, window washers, insulators, surveyors, etc. Anyone offering you a service should be considered a contractor.

You as the General Contractor

In some instances, you may want to act as your own general contractor. Many times, homeowners do this to save money. For large projects, this may not be a good idea if you are not experienced in construction trade practices. In most cases, homeowners do not know how to manage the project the way a professional general contractor would. Things overlooked, unexpected problems, scheduling conflicts, delays and/or cost overruns may end up wiping out any *"I'll do it myself"* savings.

Acting as your own contractor, there are so many things you would have to keep up with:

- Rescheduling your personal life to manage the project
- Determining what your scope of work is
- Understanding any plans drawn by an architect, engineer, drafting firm, etc.
- Finding, screening and scheduling all subcontractors
- Contracting with each subcontractor individually
- Having knowledge of typical subcontractor pricing
- Pricing materials
- Obtaining all permits necessary for the work
- Making sure everything is built to code
- Obeying all relevant construction laws
- Ordering materials, scheduling deliveries, confirming products delivered
- Overseeing and supervising workers for time schedule adherence
- Making daily phone calls to schedule work in order of necessity
- Juggling when one issue throws everything off schedule
- Being flexible for unexpected problems and delays
- Making sure job safety is the number one priority
- Getting all necessary inspections and approvals
- Paying workers
- Etc., Etc.

As an owner/builder, you may be exempt from state contractor licensing requirements for yourself, but those exemptions require that you actively supervise the project. If you act as your own general contractor, you remain legally obligated and responsible to comply with state laws, including applicable building codes. If you hire workers directly, you may also have obligations for certain compliance with labor laws, workers' compensation insurance matters, health and workplace safety regulations, liability insurance, medical insurance, employment taxes, legal minimum wage and overtime pay issues. If you are not in accordance with the issues listed above, you may be legally (and financially) responsible in the event of an accident, non-compliance or performance failure on the job. You may also be fined and could possibly face criminal penalties.

This is an area where a construction attorney or trusted legal advisor can help you determine if you want to act as your own general contractor.

Now that you've determined you are going to hire a general contractor instead of becoming one, let's find a contractor.

Finding a Contractor

NCPHIF always shouts from the rooftop: "NOT ALL CONTRACTORS ARE BAD!" Most contractors are honest and competent tradesmen with solid reputations, offering quality workmanship and fairly priced services. Let's also add that honest and competent contractors may not be the cheapest, in part because they take the time and money to abide by all laws, regulations, and professional standards while giving great service.

There are, however, dishonest contractors who go to great lengths to take your hard-earned money and not provide the services promised or if they do, they perform shoddy work. Unfortunately, they don't come to your house with shirts labeled *con artist.* Contractors who are dishonest unfairly compete with honest contractors who stand behind their work, comply with applicable laws and maintain all applicable licenses and education requirements.

So where do you find a qualified contractor? A trade organization? The Yellow Pages? Third party referral services? The Internet? Referrals from family or friends? An ad in the church bulletin? The guy you see working on your neighbor's house? In the end, it doesn't matter. What does matter is once you find one, it's extremely important that YOU conduct your own background check before you hire him.

Note: Be sure to choose a contractor who specializes in the work you need done.

Trade Organizations

As an unbiased nonprofit, we do not recommend contractors. However, NCPHIF suggests homeowners reach out to longstanding trade associations for information when looking for a service provider. Professional trade association members are generally required to conform to specific legal business operations and quality of performance standards, not just pay a membership fee.

The **National Association of the Remodeling Industry (NARI)** and the **National Association of Home Builders (NAHB)** have been reliable and scrupulous referral sources. There are associations for almost every trade in existence. Active members in these associations invest time and energy to increase their business as well as their knowledge base of construction issues.

Some companies may join an association just to have that association's logo on their website so verify that the contractor is an active member and find out what contractors have to do to become a member. Many professional associations have certifications which they require their members to complete (*i.e., continuing education classes, perform required hours of specialized work, pass a competency test, etc.*).

Some contractors may have titles that include the word *"certified"* (*certified remodeler, certified green professional, etc.*) or other *designation* titles. You may see these titles (or initials) on business cards or on websites. Look them up. Ask about them. Understand what they mean and how contractors get them.

Many professional associations also have a code of ethics. Unfortunately, the worst case punishment for a violation may be a loss of membership. Ask the association how they handle non-compliant members or complaints against members.

Insurance Companies' Preferred Contractor Lists

Insurance companies usually maintain lists of preferred contractors. Although no one, not even an insurance company, can guarantee a contractor's work performance, they do have a vested interest in providing reliable contractors.

Even insurance companies may not realize that one of their preferred contractors is underperforming if no one reports it. In fact, if you are having a problem with a contractor who was recommended by your insurance company, be sure to alert them. The contractor may be removed from the list if he fails to comply with performance or business operating standards. Contractors value their position on these preferred lists and usually work to make things right when something goes wrong.

Third Party Referral Services

Some consumers use **third-party referral services** to identify and select a contractor. There are many third party referral services, some large, some small, some national and some local. Some charge you to be a member; others may not. Some "reviews" may be fictional, some legitimate. But how can you tell? There is no guarantee the contractor's licensing, insurance coverage or other credentials were verified by that referral service. Even if they did verify the credentials, are they in the same good standing today? Ultimately, the responsibility to appraise and select a qualified contractor rests on you and not the referral service.

Contractor Marketing

Be cautious of flashy websites or flyers you receive in your mailbox. Many of these marketing materials are perfectly legit, but some illicit contractors will provide false and misleading materials. Dishonest and unethical contractors can pay a few thousand dollars to have a fancy website created, to give the impression that they are established and reputable operators. In some cases, the photos used may not even be the work of that contractor. Customer reviews may have been actually created by the contractor. This isn't the case with every contractor who has a website. We just want you to be aware.

Selecting a contractor on the singular basis of a listing in a phone book or a mailer delivered to your home does not mean that these contractors aren't reputable. But it doesn't mean they are either.

Emotionally Attached Contractors

More often than not, homeowners use a contractor recommended by someone they know. Sometimes the contractor is a friend of a friend, your friend or even a family member. They may be the deacon from your church or even your pastor (*yes, we've had homeowners who were scammed by their pastors*) or your husband's best friend or your cousin's boyfriend. We call these types of recommendations *"emotionally attached"* service providers.

You must conduct the same level of due diligence in screening any and all individuals you are entering into a business relationship with, regardless of who recommended them. Exercising smart business decisions and financial control of your funds, regardless of personal history or relationship, is a wise fraud prevention measure. Some victims have reported that close friends, family members and trusted associates have committed some of the worst construction nightmares.

When you hire a family member or friend, your *emotional attachment* will be different than if you hire a contractor you don't know.

Without an objective assessment of their business proficiency, skills and professional integrity, you are putting yourself in a vulnerable position. Hiring friends, family members or other individuals with whom you have an *emotional* relationship can end up costing you money, destroyed relationships and major tension with family and/or friends if it doesn't go right.

Regardless of where you find a contractor, you must still do your homework and check them out. Trust the guy? Okay, but verify! Like the guy? Okay, but verify! Believe the guy? Okay, but verify!

Contacting Contractors

When you find contractors who interest you, you are now ready to have them come look at your project to give you an estimate and/or quote of what labor needs to be performed, what materials/supplies need to be purchased, how long the job will take, and how much it will cost. Before you allow these strangers into your home, we recommend some safety tips.

Safety Issues Before the Potential Contractor Arrives

Before you allow a contractor into your home, be sure to put away anything of value, such as expensive jewelry, information with your social security number on it, bank statements or travel information. You may have personal information on your computer, so log off before the contractor gets to your home. Don't give anyone a reason to return or mention to cohorts when you will be away from home.

If at all possible, have someone with you when the contractor comes to your home. Ladies and seniors, this is for you, especially. You never want to seem as vulnerable as you really are. Consider these prospective contractors as complete strangers. Call a friend, neighbor, relative, maybe someone from your church, to stay with you while you have contractors in your home preparing estimates or quotes. If you cannot find anyone, ask if your community has a *neighborhood watch* or *community policing* program that can assist you so that you are not alone when contractors come to your home. Aside from the safety issue, it is helpful to have a trusted friend there who can listen with a little less emotional involvement. They may hear or see things that you may not pick up on.

Before you allow any contractors into your home, take a minute and write down the license plate number and a detailed description of their vehicle. Take a picture of the individual and his vehicle then text or email that information to someone. If you don't have access to texts or emails, call someone and give them the contractor's information over the phone. NCPHIF has been told by law enforcement that their inability to pursue scammers is because homeowners only have a vague description of the perpetrator.

If a contractor asks you if you live alone, always answer "***no***." This is none of their business and has nothing to do with the work you need done.

Getting Estimates and Quotes

Note: The terms "*estimates*" and "*quotes*" are often interchangeable. Keep that in mind. The typical differences are described below.

Estimates

The first thing you need a contractor to do is to give you an **estimate**. Estimates give you an idea of what the job will cost. You can get estimates over the phone or have a contractor do a quick walk through and tell you what they think the job will cost. You can get as many estimates as you like, so you have a good idea of how much your project will probably cost. Always get at least 3 estimates. You won't know the typical price of the project with just one estimate.

Also, pay attention to their work ethic. When you called them, did they return the call promptly? When they came to do a quick walk through, were they on time?

CHECKLIST: Estimates	
Contractor/Salesperson's Name:	
Contractor's/Salesperson's Telephone Number:	
Company Name (*as registered with state*):	
Rough Estimate (*price/amount*) he quoted me	$_____
Does this contractor specialize in the work I need done?	
How many years of experience does he have?	
Is this contractor licensed? (*business license? Where applicable, contractor's license?*)	
Is this contractor insured, bonded? (*general liability and workers' compensation, types of bonds*)	
Did he return my call promptly or show up on time?	
Did I feel good about our conversation? Will I consider inviting him to give me a formal quote?	

Now that you have an idea of what it will cost, and it fits within your budget (*what you can afford*), it is time to get **quotes**.

Quotes

Quotes are very detailed reports of what your project is, what labor and materials/supplies will be necessary, how long the job will take, who will be doing the job, how much it will cost, etc. Quotes should also include down payment amounts, finance charges, the cost of any necessary taxes, permitting fees, tear down/rip up costs, debris removal, insurance costs, etc. They should also include any extra funds needed in case any problems arise during the job.

You can choose from the contractors who gave you estimates, or you can choose someone you haven't contacted yet, to give you quotes. But do a quick screening of these contractors so you don't waste your time (*or theirs*) having them come to your home to give you a detailed scope of work only to discover that they are not properly licensed in your state or don't have adequate insurance coverage. Look them up in your state's corporations division (Secretary of State) to confirm they are licensed to do business in your state. Keep in mind, the contractor may have a perfectly legitimate license in another state, but not in your state. He should be licensed in your state.

Quotes need to be IN WRITING. Any contractor who will not provide this information to you in writing and in detail is not the contractor for you.

Before we go any further into the topic of getting quotes, here are some *do's* and *don'ts* you should know:

- **Do** get *at least three quotes.* Getting three quotes is standard but not a law. You may get as many quotes as you like, but *always* get at least three. This way, you can compare *"apples to apples."* This will allow you to see if a contractor forgot to add something or added something extra that the others did not. This is a great way to learn exactly what is needed for your project. This also gives you the opportunity to ask the contractor questions about his quote, which will give you a better feel about his experience and personality.

Note: You may really like the first contractor or salesperson who comes to give you an estimate or quote and want to hire him on the spot. But be warned, if you use the first person you meet, you are at risk of being overcharged. Get at least two other quotes to compare. You can always use the contractor who most strongly appealed to you after you get more quotes.

- **Do** compare the quotes you get. Is there a full scope of work in each quote? A **Scope of Work** is everything that has to be done on the project and who is going to do it (*labor*), every item that has to be purchased to do the job (*materials/supplies*), and all the particulars of the job (*warranties, taxes and fees, finance charges, upfront deposits, etc.*). The Scope of Work should list every single thing that involves labor, including permits, tear up, debris removal, clean up, installation, etc., as well as all the professionals/workers necessary to do the job. It should list every material/supply needed, including any equipment to be used.

  A piece of paper with the words *"new roof"* or *"as required"* does not constitute a full or definitive Scope of Work. If a quote does not have a full Scope of Work, ask that they provide it. If they refuse because *"it's too much work"* (*or any other excuse*), tell them thank you and send them on their way. Providing detailed quotes should be their cost of doing business. On the other hand, you should understand that you are costing the contractor his time, so it is important to know as much as possible in advance so you can get straight to the point with him and not have him spend his time unnecessarily. Remember, in all fairness, he is in business to make money.

- **Do** tell the contractor of any particular items, brands, models, colors, etc. you want installed so they can all bid on the same things. One who bids on oak cabinets and block countertops will have a different bid from one who bids on mahogany cabinets and Italian marble countertops. You get the picture.

- **Don't** tell the contractor what your budget is. How much he charges to do the work should have nothing to do with how much money you have. For example, if you tell him your budget is $80,000, how much do you think he is going to charge you for the job? Expect him to ask *"so, what's your budget?"* Tell him *"let's not worry about that right now. I just want to know what you will charge me to install these cabinets I picked out"* or *"I haven't set a budget yet. I just want to get an idea about the costs involved so I can see what my options are."*

- **Don't** be talked into signing any quotes at the beginning stages of your evaluation and decision-making. Don't let a quote become a contract because you signed it. At the point you are ready to sign a contract, there is much more to consider than just what is in a quote. If you sign something without fully understanding what it is, you could be obligating yourself to exclusively use that contractor or pay him if you don't.

  Note: Many contracts expressly state that any "promises" quoted by the salesperson, which are not actually written into the contract are not a part of the contract. That's why you must read everything.

Now that the contractor is here to give you a quote:

Pay attention to any red flags about their personality. Are they anxious? Frustrated with your questions? Pushy? Do they smell like alcohol? Wear sunglasses and won't remove them? Did they show up on time? When you begin a relationship with a contractor, you at least want to feel good about the person you may choose to spend the next several weeks with and give your money to. Listen to your instincts. However, don't let your instincts be a substitute for a thorough background check. Always remember, many have very charming personalities!

Make sure you accompany any person around your home while they are making an assessment to provide a quote. Do not let them out of your sight. Your attentiveness will make it difficult for them to "create" more problems. Try to make all phone calls and use the bathroom before the contractor comes to give you a quote, so you can stay with him during the assessment.

> **NCPHIF TIP:** Do not show a contractor a competing quote until AFTER he has given you his bid. If a bidder knows you already have, say, two quotes at $10,000, he may charge you $9,500 instead of what he planned to charge you ($9,000) before he saw the other bids.

You should always request a **fixed price quote** which gives you a bottom line price of what the job will cost. Sometimes, however, a contractor may propose a **cost plus quote** if he feels like there might be more to the job than meets the eye, like problems that may be behind a wall. He wants to protect himself from a fixed price if he has to do extensive work after he rips the wall out and discovers a huge problem. If he does this, make sure he gives you a maximum price on what it will cost. Don't leave the door wide open for him to continue racking up charges.

> **Note:** If subcontractors are required, they should be listed by name with license and insurance information on the quote. If the contractor doesn't have that information when he gives you a quote, that's okay. But make sure it is in your contract if you later decide to hire him.

Now that you are aware of some do's and don'ts when getting quotes, when the contractor comes to your home to give you a quote (*it should be in writing*), get as much of the information below as possible.

(*If you don't already have a "CHECKLIST: Estimates" on any contractors who are giving quotes, be sure to capture that CHECKLIST information also.*)

CHECKLIST:
Quotes

Salesperson's Name:	
Salesperson's Telephone Number:	
Company Name (*as registered with state*):	
Physical Street Address (*not a post office box*):	
Office Telephone Number:	
Cell Phone Number:	
Fax:	
Email:	
Website Address:	
Price Quoted:	
Does price quoted include all code requirements, taxes, fees, etc.?	
Is this a fixed price quote?	

Are you providing me a Full Scope of Work?	
Does the quote include the costs for tear down/rip up, clean up, permit fees, insurance, debris removal, etc?	
Does the quote include any extra costs for unexpected problems?	
Do you foresee any possible problems that may arise during the project (*behind walls, etc.*)?	
How much deposit do you require up front? What is that deposit for?	
What forms of payment do you accept?	
List All Subcontractors who will be used	
Additional Information:	

Just copy the worksheet above for each additional quote.

You are now at the point where you've obtained three (or more) quotes, which should give you sufficient information to make your decision. The quotes should be close in price. If a quote is significantly lower or higher than the others, that should be a yellow flag to ask more questions. Neither the cheapest nor the most expensive quote may equate to quality of performance. Remember the old adages *"you get what you pay for"* and *"if you can't tell the difference, why pay the difference."* So be careful, don't base selection of your contractor solely on the bid price.

Compare the quotes. Is there a full **Scope of Work** in each quote? If a quote does not have a full Scope of Work, toss it. Is the information in the quotes similar to each other? If there is a significant difference, ask the contractor to explain what it is or why it is. Within reason, your quotes should clearly allow *"apples to apples"* comparison. If they are vastly different (*"apples to oranges"*) and you are uncomfortable trying to figure out which is the best quote, remember you can also ask questions online, visit your local retailer, or contact your local homebuilder's association or a construction inspector to get a better understanding of what is being presented in the bids you received.

Having met with each prospective contractor and reviewed and compared their quotes, you're almost ready to decide who to hire. Eliminate the contractor(s) you are uncomfortable with. If you are not comfortable with them now, you probably won't be later.

> **NCPHIF TIP:** Remember many homeowners say that the contractor who ripped them off *"appeared really nice and honest."* Sometimes, at the estimating and/or quoting stage, you may be dealing with a salesperson, not the contractor who is actually going to do the work. Let the salesperson know early in the process that you want to meet the on site team leader before you sign any contract. If he or she doesn't agree, don't use them. Remember, you're the boss! It's your property.

✓ CHECKLIST: Quote Summary				
Name of Contractor	Scope of Work Attached to Quote?	Years of Experience	Licensed and Insured (Yes/No)	Price Quote
Quote 1:				
Quote 2:				
Quote 3:				
Quote ___:				
Quote ___:				

The Screening Process

Now that you have met with all the contractors and gotten their quotes, you can eliminate any contractors you are not interested in working with. Once you determine which contractors you are interested in, it is time to do background checks on each of them, regardless of whether you have decided on the one you want to do the work or cannot decide between two or three. The background check may make the decision for you.

Background Checks

You don't have to check the background of every contractor who gives you a quote. But checking the background of any contractors under final consideration is a must. We have received countless calls from homeowners who later discovered their contractor was a sex offender, had a criminal record, already scammed other homeowners, etc.

Keep in mind there are many great contractors out there and they do not mind when you ask for information to do a background check on them.

> **Note:** Remember, some may still be dishonest people with clean backgrounds. Just because you get a favorable background report does not mean the contractor is honest. It may just mean he hasn't been caught yet!

It is easy to create *official-looking* documents using today's sophisticated software programs and quality printers. You can be easily tricked especially when you do not know what a contractor's license or other documents look like. You can go online and find a most recent sample of a contractor's license for your state or you can contact us. When you get information from the contractor (*i.e., insurance information, license information, etc.*) make sure you <u>verify</u> all of it. Here are some things to check:

Always get the contractor's full name and the exact legal name of the business (*as registered with the state*). Ask to see their driver's license to confirm they are who they say they are. If they won't give you this, you may not want to use them.

The contractor may give you a post office box number or a business address that doesn't actually exist. It may look like a street address but it may be just a drop box in a mail service storefront. Contractors with showrooms or offices will typically have those identified as the principal place of business. You can always do a drive by to further confirm that the business actually exists. You may also be able to use an online mapping service (*like Google Earth or Bing Maps*) to see the address.

> **Note:** Sometimes, contractors work out of their homes and may use a post office box or other address in order to keep their home address private (*which may help avoid putting their families at risk*). Ideally, though, you want to ask them for their home address if they work out of a home office.

Ascertain how long the contractor has been in business under the name of that particular business entity. Many contractors go out of business or change their name within three to five years because of bad management and/or consumer complaints. So chances are, if a business entity has the same business name for five or more years, is in good standing with the Secretary of State, and has appropriate licenses, insurance and references, they might be a good candidate to consider. If they've just incorporated two weeks ago, you need to take that into consideration. That doesn't necessarily mean they are dishonest, just not well established in the community yet.

Business License vs. Contractor's License

Your question to a contractor who says "*I am licensed*" should be "*licensed how?*"

- **Business License:** A business license is different from a contractor's license. Almost ALL businesses must have a business license. It does not mean that the service provider is specifically licensed to do building trades work. Getting a business license just means they are licensed to do business in your state. In most circumstances, a business license is merely an occupational tax license to evidence that the business paid the required tax to the local government for doing business in that jurisdiction. Verify the contractor's business license. Have them give you the exact, legal name of their business, then verify that the business license is active and compliant with your state's corporation office (Secretary of State).

- **Contractor's License:** Some states require a general contractor to have a contractor's license. Contact your local building department to ask if your project requires the service provider to have a state contractor's license. Contact your state licensing agency and find out what a contractor has to do to get a contractor's license. Does he have to have general liability insurance? Workers' compensation insurance? Does he have to pass a competency exam? Provide financial information? Obtain a bond? Perform so many hours of work? Have to take continuing education classes? This will really help you understand the level of experience a licensed contractor has under his belt. If your project does require a special license, don't use any contractor who doesn't have it.

Sometimes a state may not require the contractor have a contractor's license; however they may require them to register with the state (**contractor registration**). Your local building department can tell you if this is the case in your jurisdiction.

More often than not, plumbers, electricians and heating/air contractors have to have a special contractor's license in their state. Verify with your local building department or licensing agency that these subcontractors are licensed and in good standing. The **National Association of State Contractors Licensing Agencies (www.nascla.org)** is a great source to answer any questions you may have.

Note: Whenever possible, always work with a licensed contractor. In some states, if you hire an unlicensed contractor, you may be subject to pay a civil penalty for aiding and abetting unlicensed activity.

Adequate Insurance Coverage

When you are gathering information about a contractor, make sure he has proof of **general liability insurance** and **workers' compensation coverage**. Verify that the coverage is sufficient and that the insurance policy is valid (*active and compliant*) and will not expire during your project. You can do this by calling the contractor's insurance company listed on the Certificate of Insurance. Even though their insurance papers indicate they are covered for the next couple of months, if they do not pay the monthly premiums, they may not have coverage at all. That is why it is so important to verify any information the contractor provides. Here is where your insurance agent can be a great resource.

Note: Don't feel like you are "bothering" your personal insurance agent if you need any help. You are paying them to advise you on insurance issues. Use them!

Legal and Criminal Claims

You can augment your search by checking online for complaints and lawsuits by or against the contractor or subcontractor(s). Some counties have court records online. Check the county of the contractor's principal place of business to see what lawsuits may have been brought, now or recently. This information is usually public. You can also check the lien history with your county property assessor's office or similar agency. Keep in mind that most contractors may have some litigation history or lien history, and that's normal. You are reviewing their history to learn if it is *excessive*.

Building Department

You can check with your local building department for information on a contractor. You can find out if his license is current and active. Many times, you can find out his inspection history, such as how many times he had to get something re-inspected. If it is excessive, this may be a sign that he performs shoddy construction. This is not always the case, but it is something to consider.

> **NOTE: Disclosure statements** are documents that list the contractor's license number and confirm that he is bonded. Check with your state's licensing board or local building department to determine if your contractor should provide you with a disclosure statement.

Contractor Background Check

The worksheet below provides various background checks (*questions*) you should know about any contractor you are considering. You do not have to ask him every question; we just wanted to present you with some options. *(If you have good questions not listed here, please send them to* **www.PreventContractorFraud.org** *so we can pass that information on to others!)*

CHECKLIST: Contractor Background Check	Your Notes
What is the Legal Name of you and your company:	
What is your physical address?	
What is your office phone number? Cell phone number? After hours phone number? Emergency phone number?	
What is your Business License Number: Is the company active and compliant? (*This will be verified with the Secretary of State*)	
How long have you been in business?	
How long (*how many years*) have you been listed with the Secretary of State?	

Have you operated under any other trade/business names? If so, what names and in what states?	
Contractor's Specialty: What projects do you specialize in?	
How long have your employees and/or subcontractors worked with you?	
Do you have any certifications/designations? If so, what certifications and with who?	
What percentage of your customers are repeat business?	
What percentage of your customers are from referrals?	
What is your current rating with the Better Business Bureau?	

What is your state Contractor's License number (*if applicable*)? Is your license active and compliant? Have you ever been cited for any violations?	
Can you provide a copy of your current insurance policy? Is your policy active and valid as of today's date? Date: _____ What is the name and contact phone number of your insurance company? Will the policy be valid throughout the entire project? Do you have general liability insurance? How much liability coverage? Do you have workers' compensation insurance?	
Are you bonded? If so, what type of bonds and what is the name and contact information of your bonding company?	
Where applicable, can you provide a Disclosure Statement?	
Do you have any criminal records (*criminal or otherwise*)? If so, please briefly explain.	
What trade organizations are you a member of? How long have you been a member of each trade organization?	

Please list at least two suppliers that you work with regularly and their contact information.	
Have you ever had previous licenses under different names? If so, what names, and why?	
Have you ever had any disciplinary action and/or claims filed against you or your company? If so, what happened and how was it resolved?	
Have you had any legal claims (*lawsuits*) filed against you or your company? If so, what happened and how was it resolved?	
How many projects do you typically handle at the same time?	
How many projects have you completed in the past two years that were similar to this job?	
How do you resolve situations when your customers are not happy with your services?	
Is there anything else you would like us to know to consider hiring you for this project?	

Now that you have gotten the information from the contractor, here are some things you need to do with that information:

NCPHIF highly recommends you consider conducting additional research through diverse, credible organizations (*Better Business Bureau, your local Chamber of Commerce, your Secretary of State's office, State Attorney General's office, state licensing agencies, consumer protection agencies, and your local law enforcement*) to determine if any complaints have been filed against any contractor you are considering.

When you check the Better Business Bureau (BBB) in your state to see if there are any complaints against the contractor, be sure to check with the BBB in surrounding states as well. The contractor may have scammed several people in another state and no one in your state....yet!

If the contractor admits to a criminal record, research further. They may tell you about a DUI they got last year but not how they were charged with stealing jewelry from a previous customer.

If the contractor lists trade organizations which he belongs to, contact those trade organizations and confirm how long he has been a member. Also ask the trade organizations -- what does it take to be a member? Only pay a fee? Perform over 250 hours of work? Take code of ethics classes? Be licensed in their field? If contractor's only have to pay a fee to be a member, keep in mind, anyone can do that.

Once the contractor lists suppliers (*electricians, material supplier, lumberyard, other businesses, etc.*) that he works with regularly, contact them and ask if the contractor pays them on time. How long have they had a relationship with the contractor?

Now keep this important point in mind: a contractor's past performance may not always be a reliable indication of whether he is going to perform as well as he has in the past. There are many factors that may bring a change in his performance or business practices. The company may have had a good reputation in the past; however, today the company may be insolvent, failing to pay suppliers and/ or workers, or operating without the proper licenses and insurance coverage. The contractor may have complaints filed against him for dishonest or suspicious dealings in his operation. He may be distracted by personal or other issues, like drug or gambling addictions or devastating medical costs. Keep up with his current situation and current referrals as best you can.

References

Checking references is another step to bring you closer to making a final decision in selecting your contractor. Consider asking for references from customers who were not happy at first, but will tell you how the problem was resolved to their satisfaction. Another alternative is to ask for references from the three to five most recent jobs which may prevent the contractor from *cherry picking* the best jobs over the last several years.

Remember, you can obtain as many references as you wish. Keep in mind that while this is a great way to get more information about the contractor and their work, it is not foolproof. Chances are, a contractor is only going to give you good references, or they may have friends/family give them excellent references even though no work was done. In these days, more often than not, other customers are not comfortable with you (*someone they don't know*) visiting their homes to see the contractor's work. You don't have to capture all the information below, but you should try to get feedback for most of it.

CHECKLIST:
References

Date Reference Checked:	
Name of Reference:	
City and State:	
Phone:	
Email:	
Job Performed:	
Date Started and Completed:	
Was Job Completed on Time:	
Was Job Completed to Reference's Satisfaction:	
Rating on a Scale of 1-10 (*10 being the highest rank*):	
How did you locate this contractor?	
Did he request an upfront deposit? If so, how much?	
Were there any unexpected costs?	
Were you displeased with anything?	
Did he return phone calls in a timely manner?	
How did contractor respond to complaints/problems?	
Would you use this contractor again?	
Would you be okay if I came by to see his work? (*If so, get address*)	

NCPHIF TIP: Be careful. If you ever refer a contractor, always advise your neighbors to do their own background checks. You may also want to caution them not to give money up front. Scammers are known to perform model/demo projects only to collect monies up front for other jobs in the area, then skip town without beginning and/or completing the work for the other homeowners, leaving them to suspect that you may have been in on the scam because you referred them. Not a good feeling when your neighbors think you are a cheat!

Whew! We know you are probably exhausted by now. Finding and screening contractors is a lot of work. Nonetheless, they are necessary steps to help you avoid getting ripped off by a scam artist. Background checks and comprehensive screenings are effective ways to minimize as many issues as possible before you hire anyone.

Most fraud victims who contact us are upset with themselves for not spending more time scrutinizing the contractor before they hired them. They tell us they have been suffering for months, and sometimes years, trying to correct the problem or recover lost money! It doesn't take months or years to screen a contractor before you hire him.

Selecting the Contractor

Now that you have gotten estimates, quotes, references and background checks, it is time for you to select the contractor you want to hire to do your job. Be sure to listen to your instincts as well as your intellect.

If you don't feel any of the contractors are right for your job, you don't have to hire them. Get new quotes. It may require a little extra time, but you want to make sure you have the right person for the job.

Once you've selected the contractor you want to use, there are a few things you need to handle before he begins any work.

CHAPTER 5

Before the Project

Man in the Mirror

Now that you have selected your contractor, you need to sit down with him and go over everything. This will help cut down on any miscommunication. But before you ask him questions, you need to first ask yourself a few:

CHECKLIST: Man In the Mirror	Yes/No
Am I going to commit to being my own quality control manager for the project?	
Can I be reasonable and let him get the work done without calling him every second?	
Am I going to be reasonable about unexpected costs that come up?	
Am I okay with my contractor making a profit to manage this job?	
Will I be flexible if the job takes longer than expected?	
Do family and friends tell me my expectations are always too high?	
Am I going to pay him when he is finished and gives me everything I need based on our contract?	

It is always a good idea to talk to the person in the mirror. That's who you need to have the first meeting of the minds with.

Meeting of the Minds

Now that you have had a heart-to-heart with yourself, here are some things you and your contractor need to meet about so both of you are clear on these issues. Feel free to ask questions that may not be listed here if they are a concern to you. Ask as many questions as you want. Now is the best time to do it, before anything is signed or any work begins. In home repair projects, there is frequent miscommunication because the parties involved have not had a meeting of the minds. Once these details are ironed out, they need to be included in your contract, which we will discuss later.

CHECKLIST: Meeting of the Minds	
Project Start Date: What day will the project start?	
What will the hours be? Days? Are you working on weekends? When will you break for lunch?	
Project Completion Date: What is the actual date the project will be completed?	
If applicable, do you have a copy of architect/engineer plans, approvals, etc.?	
Contact Person for the Project: (*This is usually the general contractor but can be anyone you both agree to.*)	
How often will the contractor be on site?	

Contractor's Emergency Contact: If you call the contractor, he will respond within how many hours? What about calling after hours if there is a problem/emergency?	
You have a list of everyone who will be working on this project, by name, company name, expertise, dates they will be on the project, etc.?	
Has the contractor confirmed he will obtain all permits in connection with this project? What permit(s) are necessary for the project?	
Full Scope of Work (*in detail*): (*This can be the quote he provided. Just make sure it is referenced in and made a part of the contract.*)	
Required Equipment: What equipment will be needed? If that equipment is rented by the contractor, who is he renting the equipment from? What days will it be used? When will it be returned?	
Exact Materials to be Used: (*These should be outlined in the Full Scope of Work provided on the quote, to be attached to and made part of your contract.*)	
Will the contractor's employees do some of the work? If so, which employees and what work?	

What work will be subcontracted?	
How many subcontractors will be working on the property? (*If subs will be working on your property, you need a complete list of those subcontractors and their credentials before they work on your home. See 'Subcontractors' section below.*)	
Do you have written confirmation from the contractor that he has done a thorough and comprehensive background check on each subcontractor?	
Do all subcontractors have appropriate insurance coverage? Do they have proper licensing?	
Description of what exactly constitutes **"Substantial Completion"** for this job.	
How often will he communicate with you as the job progresses? Daily meetings at the end of the day? Daily meetings first thing in the morning? Weekly meetings? (*You decide, you're the boss!*)	
What is the contractor's plan for unforeseen problems? Has he included an allowance for such in his pricing?	

What is his approach to problem solving and resolving any complaints you may have?	
Does the contractor understand that you will require lien waivers/releases (*explained later*) before each payment? Does he have any issues with providing you with lien waivers/releases?	
Is he going to stay on top of weather forecasts to protect the job?	
Are there any special instructions if you have children or pets? Certain working hours?	
Terms of Any and All Warranties/ Guarantees: Does it transfer if we sell our home? Does it require any maintenance on our part? Exactly what does the warranty cover and what does it not cover? If there is a material warranty, does it cover the labor it will take to replace the defective materials?	
Is additional contractor's insurance required to cover specifics (*i.e., equipment rental, etc.*)?	

Name and Contact Information of Contractor's Bond Company:	
Do you and the contractor agree on the payment schedule? (*The payment schedule MUST be detailed in your contract.*)	
Does the contractor agree to give you copies of all invoices?	
What does the contractor require of you during the project?	
Other:	

Subcontractors

In many cases, the general contractor will hire subcontractors (*plumbers, electricians, etc.*) to handle or help with your project. You might assume the subcontractors and/or crew members on your project are your contractor's staff or employees. This is not always the case.

Subcontractors are frequently separate independent business persons, but in some cases, they may include day workers picked from a pool of unemployed people standing on the street. As many news stories have revealed, the general contractor most likely did not conduct background screenings on temporary workers hired. Some day laborers may be undocumented workers, or may be drug addicts, thieves, etc., which poses a security risk for you.

Keep in mind however, more often than not, individuals *standing on the street* are good guys just looking for work so they can feed their families and aren't a threat. The problem is: how do you tell the difference between them and the bad guys? This is about protecting yourself, your family, and everything in your home. What preventive measures can you take?

You need to know exactly who is coming into your home, and that includes subcontractors. Require the contractor provide you a complete list of the people he'll be using on your project. The contractor should be able to provide written confirmation that he conducted comprehensive and thorough background checks – especially criminal history verification -- on all the people he'll bring on the project and into your home.

You also need confirmation that every subcontractor is licensed, where applicable, and has appropriate insurance coverage. What happens if a subcontractor falls off your roof? Who is responsible? You need to know that information.

Here is some information you may want to get before you allow sub-contractors in your home. Remember, you can capture as little or as much information as you deem necessary for your project.

CHECKLIST:
Subcontractor Information

Subcontractor Name:	
Subcontractor Company Name:	
Subcontractor Company Address:	
Subcontractor Representative:	
Subcontractor Address:	
Subcontractor Telephone:	
Subcontractor Fax:	
Subcontractor Email:	
Subcontractor Website:	
Subcontractor Insurance Information:	
What part of the work will be done by this subcontractor?	
How long will this subcontractor be on the project? (*Number of days*)	
Has the subcontractor provided a copy of an active compliant state license?	
Has the subcontractor provided a copy of his insurance certificate?	
Does the subcontractor understand that you will request lien waivers to be signed?	
Did the general contractor authorize this subcontractor to work on this project?	
Date subcontractor is to start their portion of the project:	
Date subcontractor is to finish their portion of the project:	

You can copy this form for each subcontractor who will be working on your project.

Now that you know everyone who is going to step foot on your property, there are just a few more things you should know. Now is a good time to discuss building permits, payment schedules, materials, warranties, and other things related to the project. These items should be discussed and agreed to by you and the contractor BEFORE you sign anything. These things should also be detailed in your contract.

Building Permits

A **building permit** or **construction permit**, is a permit that most jurisdictions require for many construction projects. A permit requires the project to be inspected, usually during and after construction, to make sure that the work is in compliance with all building code requirements. If you fail to get a permit when one is required, you may have to pay significant fines and penalties. Sometimes your project may have to be torn down if it does not meet code requirements. Wouldn't it be awful to have to tear down a project you paid to have done, just because no one got the proper permits?

Unless you are skilled in the construction industry, think long and hard about obtaining the building permit yourself. If you obtain the permit, you may be responsible for, among other things: code violations, inspections, insurance coverage, workers' compensation, legal liability for the quality of work if someone is injured, damage to your neighbors' property resulting from the work being done on your property, taxes, etc.

The contractor should *"pull"* (obtain) any necessary permits to ensure everything is constructed to proper code, that inspections are scheduled and done, and that workers' compensation and other insurance is in place. Make sure that the contractor pulls the building permit(s) under the full and formal name of the business that matches the name of the business on your contract. You should request a copy of any permit(s) from the contractor before the project begins or any money is paid to him.

The contractor may tell you a building permit is not necessary for the work to be done. If you don't know or are not sure if a permit is required, contact your local building department to confirm what, if any, permits are needed for the work being done in your home. If the contractor was not honest, don't use him.

In states where contractors *must* have a contractor's license, a contractor may ask *you* to pull the permit because their contractor's license has to be active and compliant in order to pull the permit. A request for you to pull permits is a big scam in this case. Quite honestly, you may be perceived or assumed to be lying deliberately to your city/county (*and not even realize it*) about who is actually doing the work. You may also negate your ability to hold the contractor responsible.

In most jurisdictions, when building permits are required, the permits must be posted in clear view on the job site during the project until the final inspection and issuance of the Certificate of Occupancy (*discussed later*). Although a contractor should pull the permit, the ultimate responsibility still falls to the owner of the property.

Even where building codes exist, some local governments are lax when it comes to enforcement. Perhaps they don't have enough inspectors, are underfunded or simply cannot keep up with inspection requests; who knows. As a homeowner, you don't have to rely on building officials. This is why hiring an independent **code certified inspector** yourself, to confirm that the job has been done right, is a prudent and good idea. The **American Society of Home Inspectors (ASHI)** or the **National Association of Home Inspectors (NAHI)** may be good places to start looking for a code certified inspector. Be sure to ask them how an inspector becomes a member with their organization. Does he just pay a fee or does he have to jump through hoops to be a member (*such as, take code of ethics classes, pass exams, or do so many inspections, etc.*)?

Note: If you belong to a **Homeowners' Association (HOA)**, you may have to get permission from them for certain projects. They will usually have **Covenants, Conditions and Restrictions (CCRs)** that you must abide by. If you do not, they may impose fines. If you belong to a HOA, check your CCRs or contact your HOA representative for clarity.

If your local building department informs you that there are code violations, immediately notify your contractor by phone call and in writing. Make sure the contractor signs any violation forms you receive. Keep copies of all paperwork and document the date you received the notification and when you contacted the contractor.

Wouldn't it be nice to have a contractor who takes tremendous pride in his work? So much pride that he builds <u>above</u> standard code?

Notice of Lien Rights

In many cases, subcontractors and suppliers who do not have a direct contract with the owner of the project may be required to give a written preliminary **Notice of Lien Rights** (may also be called *Notice of Right to Lien or Notice to Owner*) to the homeowner if they want to retain their lien rights. This document alerts you that someone working on your home or supplying materials to your home can file a lien on your property if they are not paid. This can be a contractor, a subcontractor, supplier, or professional servicer.

NOTE: These documents include contact information, which you can use to confirm everyone has been paid before you give the contractor any more money.

Have the contractor give you copies of all invoices of materials purchased for your project. That way, if you need to, you can confirm with the material supplier(s) that all invoices were paid.

In some cases, a general contractor may not have to send you a Notice of Lien Rights since you already know that he is working for you, because you contracted with him directly.

Notice of Commencement (NOC)

Note: Starting work for which a permit is needed BEFORE applying for the required permit is generally unlawful and may be punishable by a fine as well as additional fees.

In some states, a **Notice of Commencement (NOC)** may be required. It is a notice that alerts the public that work is being done to improve a property. You can contact your local building department to determine if a Notice of Commencement is required in your case. If it is, keep in mind it must be recorded *before* the first inspection is requested. Usually, the Notice of Commencement must also be displayed at the job site. And once it is filed, work must begin within the designated time.

Payment/Draw Schedules

He who Controls the Money, Controls the Job

You get to call the shots; it's your home and your money! The best way to protect your money is to control your money. It's that simple.

Even with a perfect contract that mutually covers and protects all parties concerned, if you give money to a contractor and he takes off with it, nothing can guarantee you'll get your money back. You may go to court and win a judgment against the contractor. However, a court judgment does not guarantee the contractor will repay you.

This is one of the most critically important issues we discuss in our workshops all over the country. Homeowners are usually in awe when we point out that even after a court judgment in the homeowner's favor, restitution still may not be paid. This is why it is important to control the money. Excuse me....YOUR money!

Note: Never pay for an entire job up front.

In most remodeling or rebuilding projects, **payment schedules/ draw schedules** will need to be created. These payment schedules MUST be outlined in your contract.

The contractor should be paid on a **performance-based schedule**, not a time-based schedule. In other words, he should not be paid every two weeks. He should be paid because he finished an agreed-to stage of the job. Do not make payments (*other than reasonable deposits you have agreed to*) to contractors before work is done to your satisfaction. In many cases, a dishonest contractor who has been paid more than the cost of the work performed, has little incentive to return to complete the work. You need to really understand your payment schedule so some dishonest contractor cannot put your payment ahead of his work!

A performance-based schedule is predicated on the contractor completing specific milestones/stages in the work being performed (*such as drywall completion or passing the electrical inspection*). It should not be based on just a *percentage of the work being completed*. Your contractor may try to get you to agree to this percentage schedule so beware! Think about it. How would you know exactly what "*25 percent*" or "*50 percent*" of the project completion is? This needs to be detailed in your contract.

Do not make any payments until any and all necessary inspections have been completed and approved by your local building official. Make sure the contractor gives you a copy of each and every inspection certificate. This way, you will know if the code compliance officer did not approve any inspections.

> **Note:** In the payment schedule included in your contract, don't just say *"pay when doors installed."* Rather, say *"pay when doors installed by contractor and inspected and approved by code compliance officer and/or you."* This is where a good construction attorney may come in handy.

You should also consider setting up a **retainage clause** in your contract. This means that you will keep (retain) a percentage (*usually 10 percent*) of each installment payment. So, at the end of the project, you should be holding that percentage of the contractor's money, until all **punch list** items are addressed and resolved (*i.e., entire job completed, passed all inspections, lien waivers/releases received, the work site is cleaned and everything has been put back in its rightful place, paint touched up, walls cleaned, trash removed, cigarette butts removed, etc.*).

Make sure this is in your contract so there is no dispute later. Your attorney can help you set up a retainage clause in your contract. Don't expect a contractor to just agree with this payment schedule. You MUST have him agree to it in writing.

Sometimes, homeowners retain a percentage for 15-30 days to make sure nothing goes wrong and everything works the way it should. If you decide to do this, it MUST be stipulated in your contract.

As an example, let's say your project costs $40,000. You agree to pay the contractor in four (4) installments and you both have agreed, in writing, to a 10 percent retainage.

Installment Payment Amount	Installment due when?	Contractor completed this installment work?	How much was paid to contractor?	Balance Due Contractor: (Retainage)
$10,000	After tear down and debris removal, inspected and approved	Yes	$9,000	$1,000
$10,000	After installation of insulation and drywall, inspected and approved	Yes	$9,000	$1,000
$10,000	After installation of shelving, flooring, electrical work, inspected and approved	Yes	$9,000	$1,000
$10,000	After job completed	Yes	$9,000	<u>$1,000</u>
AMOUNT DUE CONTRACTOR AFTER "PUNCH LIST" COMPLETED				$4,000

If for any reason they do not return to take care of the *punch list* items, then you have the $4,000 to pay someone else to finish the job.

This payment schedule MUST BE THOROUGHLY DETAILED IN YOUR CONTRACT! Otherwise, if you withhold his money for any reason, and he takes you to court or files a lien, you may lose if your contract doesn't detail the payment schedule and payment terms.

Here is a Payment Schedule worksheet that you can use. You can always add to it. And if you do, contact us and let us know of your brilliant idea! We would love to share it with others.

CHECKLIST:
Payment Schedule

Installment Amount	Tasks to be Performed	Date Task Completed/ Passed Inspection	Invoice and Lien Waiver Received from Contractor	Date Contractor Paid	Amount Paid to Contractor	Balance due Contractor

Note: Don't make a check payable to an individual or company using a nickname. Make all payments to the legal, registered company name. For example: A contractor may tell you his name is *Johnny* and he owns *Doe Construction.* When you check with the Secretary of State, you discover the contractor's legal name is *John D. Doe, Sr.* and the full legal name of the company is *John D. Doe & Sons Construction, LLC. (This is a fictitious name and does not refer to any real person or company.)*

Never give a service provider a blank check. They may have someone else cash the check for them and then deny it was a payment from you. You want the check to be cashed by the actual service provider. If for any reason the contractor does not have a bank account, and you make the check payable to someone else, annotate the check to indicate the payment is for the contractor and list their legal name and business name in the memo section of your check AND have them sign a receipt referencing the check as a payment.

Materials and Upfront Deposits

Now that you know who will be working on your home, you need to know what materials/supplies will be used. Taking precautions will help prevent the contractor from inflating the cost of materials or substituting lesser quality, lower priced items for higher priced items. Paying for materials or supplies yourself can also prevent the contractor from taking off with your money. It can also prevent the supplier from filing a lien against your property because they were not paid by the contractor.

Most reputable contractors have a credit account with their suppliers and don't need your money upfront to purchase supplies. If you give the contractor money up front, he can take off with your money and you may never see him again. In other words, you have no protection. However, if he purchases the materials and starts the job and you don't pay him, he can file a lien against your property. He is protected. See the unbalance? Something to think about when he asks you for an upfront deposit.

If you're asked to pay money up front for items that would be considered "routine" or "common" supplies, you can always meet the contractor at the local supply store and pay for the supplies in person.

If at all possible, pay by credit card because you have legal rights under federal law to dispute a charge. If you don't have a credit card, pay by check/money order. And make sure you fill out the money order completely, including your name, address, contractor's/company name and invoice number.

If you absolutely must pay by cash, make sure you get a copy of the invoice that is marked "paid" (*and references how much cash was received on what date for what services/supplies*) and that the invoice has the name of the company and address on it. That invoice should also be signed and dated by the contractor and should itemize exactly what you are paying for. This way, you have valid documentation for recourse should you ever need it. Some homeowners have even made a video of the transaction on their cell phones as a back-up.

Remember, there are exceptions to the rule of not giving money up front. For instance, if you have specialty items, such as marble from Italy, or something engraved with your initials, or an odd colored bathtub, chances are you may have to pay in advance for those items if they are nonrefundable special orders. That way, the contractor is not on the hook to cover extraordinary costs if you opt out of the project. In these situations, you should consider paying the manufacturer or supplier directly, preferably by credit card. If you must write a check, consider making it payable directly to the supplier or to both of them (*supplier and contractor*).

Note: A number of consumer advisors suggest paying 10 percent or $1,000 (*whichever is less*) as an upfront deposit. Some states limit upfront amounts a contractor can get as a down payment and giving money up front may impact other rights. Construction attorneys, your local homebuilder's association, and/or your state licensing agency should know what those limits are specific to your state.

Before writing a check to a supplier, consider verifying that the supplier exists. Also verify that the items being ordered are in stock. Obtain the exact date of delivery of your order, and request a copy of a detailed invoice. When the special order or service has been paid for, ask the supplier to give you a "paid" receipt and if possible, a lien release.

In all fairness to the contractor, sometimes they have a markup on material costs to cover overhead and other expenditures, such as having to take the time to shop for all the supplies, gas to travel to the various suppliers, physical manpower to lift many, sometimes heavy items, insurance coverage, etc. and this is fair.

Note: In many states, if you ask your contractor for invoices of all materials and the name of the material supplier(s), by law he has to provide that information to you.

Sometimes, contractors get discount pricing from suppliers for purchasing from them. Sometimes this works in your favor, and sometimes it doesn't. *In your favor:* you get a steep discount if the contractor purchases the materials from his supplier. *Not in your favor:* if that supplier does not have the item in stock, the contractor may prefer to wait until the items are in stock instead of searching other suppliers with which he does not have a relationship. In this case, there may be no incentive for the contractor to call other suppliers (competitors) who he does not have a relationship with to see if they have the items. But you can. It can come down to the issue of time versus money.

Get a receipt and invoice to verify and keep track of all purchases. This worksheet will help you keep track of your material and supply purchases.

CHECKLIST: Materials/Supplies

Item SKU/Model/ Serial Number	Description of Item	Quantity	Price per Item	Total Price	Is there a Guarantee or Warranty on the item?

Sometimes, you will have special order materials/supplies, or items too big to haul on typical trucks, requiring delivery by a specialized vehicle. To the extent possible, remain at your home when special items are delivered to your residence so you can confirm they are not damaged. Here is some information you might want to get once the supplies are delivered.

CHECKLIST: Delivery of Materials/Supplies	
Date of Delivery:	
Delivery Company's Representative:	
Delivery Company:	
Delivery Company Telephone Number:	
Description of Items Delivered:	
1.	
2.	
3.	
4.	
5.	
How was supplier paid? By contractor? Homeowner? If by homeowner, by check? Credit card?	
Items delivered were damaged and returned on _____ (date).	

A Story: When a dishonest contractor left equipment on the property of a homeowner, the homeowner had no idea who to contact to have the machinery picked up. In the meantime, the equipment company reported it stolen.

Warranties/Guarantees

Warranties and/or guarantees are quite simple to explain, but may be complex in accountability. There are basically two types of warranties: labor and manufacturer. There is also an *extended* warranty.

Labor Warranty

Labor warranties are provided by the company doing the labor. Keep in mind, this warranty is only good as long as the company is in business. Labor warranties are usually a year, sometimes two, but very rarely more than that. A 5-year warranty may just be what the contractor tells you to get you to use his services. We've had homeowners contact us who selected the contractor because he offered a 100-year labor warranty. What are the chances of him being around to honor that?!

What you want to know about your labor warranty is:

✓ CHECKLIST: Labor Warranty	
How long does it last?	
What exactly does it cover?	
What exactly does it *not* cover?	
Does the warranty require any maintenance or instructions on my part?	
Does the warranty transfer to the new owner if I sell my home?	

Manufacturer's/Material Warranty

Manufacturer's or material warranties are provided by the material company. If there is a defect in the material, the manufacturer's/material warranty kicks in.

What you want to know about your manufacturer's/material warranty is:

CHECKLIST: Manufacturer's/Material Warranty	
How long does it last?	
What exactly does it cover?	
What exactly does it *not* cover?	
Is there a warranty card that needs to be sent to the material company?	
Do they cover Acts of God?	
Does the warranty prorate based on the age of the material?	
Is the labor to replace the defective material included in the warranty, regardless of what contractor installed it?	
If they certify their installers and something goes wrong, do they also cover the labor required to repair the problem?	

Extended Warranty

Sometimes, if you want more coverage, you may agree to pay for an **extended warranty**. Ask questions of the contractor regarding extended warranties and read any documentation, especially the fine print.

Extended warranties are usually offered when the contractor installing the materials has had extensive training and is certified to install that company's materials. The company knows the contractor will install the material the correct way, so they may extend the warranty to entice you to purchase their product.

Liens and Lien Releases/Waivers

Mechanic's Liens, Workman's Liens, Subcontractor's Liens, and Materialman's (Supplier's) Liens.

A **lien** is a legal claim on your property, making it collateral against money or services owed to another person or entity. A lien(s) can be placed on your home by the general or prime contractor, sub-contractors, material/equipment suppliers, laborers, architects and engineers, etc., if they are not paid. In other words, a lien can be placed on your home by just about anyone your contractor did not pay, *even if you paid the general or prime contractor in full*!

Lien Releases (also called Lien Waivers): A lien release is your proof that the contractor has paid the supplier or subcontractor. Make sure you get lien releases signed by the person or company being paid before you give any money to the contractor and that those lien releases absolutely follow all state statutory forms and language. Your attorney or trusted legal advisor can help you with this subject. And where applicable, have lien releases notarized, to ensure that the person signing the document has been verified, cutting down on forgery and identity theft. A **notary** (also called "**notary public**") is a person legally authorized to verify that a person signing a document is the actual person. Notaries can be found everywhere; in banks, law offices, accounting offices, etc.

Lien releases typically include the amount of the payment, type of work performed, the date the labor was started and completed or the supplies/materials were received, the name of the homeowner, the address of the property, the current date, the subcontractor/supplier's name, company and signature and a notary block (*where a notary verifies the person signing the document*).

If you have a lien placed on your property, don't panic. Call an attorney or trusted advisor who specializes in lien laws. Oddly enough, many unethical contractors file liens and never intend to foreclose. Sometimes, they are upset that you filed a complaint against them so they file a lien. They may also do it to see if you'll pay twice, even if you don't have to.

You can ask your contractor to publish a **"Notice of Completion"** in the local *legal* paper, or you can do it. This starts the clock on anyone who wants to file a lien on your home. In many cases, they have to file the lien within 45 days of the Notice of Completion being published. If no Notice of Completion is published, anyone wanting to file a lien on your home may have up to one year after the project's completion. This is a good time to get a trusted advisor or attorney to tell you what is specific to your state. This is not mandatory. We just want to bring this to your attention.

> **Note:** Make sure you get a lien release each time you make a payment. A **partial release** is necessary, for instance, when you have a payment installment schedule in your contract. Each time he is given an installment payment, he should sign a partial release. Then, when he completes the next portion of the project, the cycle continues until he is to receive his final payment. At that point, he should sign a **final release**.

Depending on your state, lien laws may vary, especially when it comes to time limitations. This makes another great reason to seek the advice of a legal professional in your state, to make sure you protect yourself.

Now, you should have a great understanding of everything you want done, what it is going to cost, the contractor who is going to do the work, how he is going to do the work, how you are going to pay him and how long it is going to take. Now, all this has to be in writing.

The Contract

(The information provided herein is for your <u>general information only</u>. It is not legal advice. As we instruct throughout this book, you should obtain legal advice from an attorney in your state. The information below is provided to give you topics to discuss with your attorney.)

Now that you and the contractor have communicated and settled on all the terms of the project, it is time for the two of you to put your agreement in writing.

> **Note:** In some states, a written contract is mandatory. It should always be mandatory for you too!

The contractor is going to hand you his standard contract which is usually written in his best interest. Just because a contract is pre-printed, it doesn't mean you cannot add, delete or change it. You can make any changes you want, as long as you both agree to and sign off on those changes. Any contract you sign should address all the specifics of your project.

Listed below are some generic topics regarding what should or should not be in your contract. Depending on your state, some may or may not qualify. It's always a good idea (*and usually less expensive*) to have an attorney review your document before you sign it. After you sign the contract, you may have to pay an attorney a lot more to represent you if something goes terribly wrong.

Here are some Do's and Don'ts regarding the contract.

DO's

- **Do** always insist on a written contract for the work. Never accept an oral contract. While many times, oral contracts are considered legal, it is always your word against his.

- **Do** put the exact legal name of the contractor and the company in the contract. This is very important. If you ever have to go to court, you need the correct legal names. Contractors sometimes use nicknames and not their legal name. For example: A contractor may tell you his name is *Johnny* and he owns *Doe Construction*. When you check with the Secretary of State, you discover the contractor's legal name is *John D. Doe, Sr.* and the full legal name of the company is *John D. Doe & Sons Construction, LLC. (This is a fictitious name and does not refer to any real person or company.)*

- **Do** understand that the contractor's company may be a limited liability company (LLC) or corporation, etc. and he may not have any assets under that corporation. This may be a problem should you have any disputes. Try to get the contractor to sign the contract under his personal name also. If he doesn't want to do it, you may want to do business with someone else. Or at least, consider having him get a performance bond.

- **Do** make sure the contract is complete and includes the full Scope of Work *(labor, materials/supplies, payments/costs schedules, warranties, guarantees, change orders, "right to cancel" disclosure, taxes and fees, finance charges, upfront deposits, etc.)* and any other details specific to your job.

- **Do** make sure you list all materials you want. Indecisions can be costly down the road!

- **Do** make sure you have a list of *"Plan B"* substitutes in case any materials you want are unavailable, on back order, discontinued, out of stock, etc. If you cannot get the materials you want, what substitutions will you agree to? If you don't state this in your contract, you leave the contractor open to choose. He may have a

substitution clause in the contract that he presents to you, which states that he can substitute any materials/supplies if he cannot get the materials you want.

- **Do** state in the contract that the contractor must have appropriate insurance coverage and must maintain that coverage during the entire project. General Liability and Workers' Compensation are a must. Your insurance agent or attorney can help you with this.

- **Do** consider a **fixed contract**. This means the price will not change (*with the exception of change orders*). An attorney specializing in construction and/or contract law can help you decide if a fixed contract is best for you.

- **Do** state in the contract that the contractor agrees to and will be responsible for meeting all state workplace health and safety regulations.

- **Do** state in the contract that the contractor will comply with all governmental building codes and will provide copies of all permits and inspection results to you.

- **Do** state in the contract that the contractor is experienced with any large equipment used on the property and will remove the large equipment after the job is complete.

- **Do** add a **pending clause** to your contract if you are waiting on your insurance company to authorize payment for the work, or if you need to borrow money to finance the work. Add a clause that the contract is valid only if insurance reimbursement or financing is obtained. Be sure to consult with an attorney or trusted advisor if you need help with the proper wording.

- **Do** list in the contract the names, license numbers, contact information and insurance coverage of all subcontractors who will be in your home or on your property.

- **Do** include in your contract what happens if subcontractors don't do their work correctly. Is the general contractor responsible if the electrician wires the room incorrectly? You want to be absolutely sure who is responsible.

- **Do** include in your contract that any damage the contractor causes while on the project will be repaired by him at his expense or he agrees to pay for the damage so you can hire someone else to do the job.

- **Do** add a clause in your contract that if there are any code violations, all payments to the contractor will cease until he corrects the situation and it passes inspection. (*Get a copy of each inspection certificate showing that the inspection passed.*)

- **Do** include your payment terms and schedule in the contract. Your payment terms and schedule MUST be part of your contract. Payments should be based on work completion, not based on time.

- **Do** make sure the contract includes procedures for **change orders** (*for anything that gets added to, altered, switched or substituted after the job is in progress*). Make sure it is clearly stated that any and all change orders must be in writing, signed off on by both you and the contractor, and that you have a right to refuse any changes that are not in writing and signed by you. Make sure your contract indicates that if the change order is necessary because of the fault of the contractor, he is responsible for that cost.

Note: We strongly suggest you never make an oral agreement to changes in your project, even if it seems like the contractor is doing you a favor. Require that the contractor specify all costs related to the change(s), and detail how they will affect the previously set completion timeline already agreed to in your contract. You want to make sure you have everything in writing in case that *"extra"* work causes problems or voids your manufacturer's warranty. Or later when problems occur, he cannot say *"it's not in the contract"* or it was *"just a favor."*

Note: If a contractor proceeds to do work, even if a change order is not signed, it may be possible for him to obtain payment under **quantum meruit**. *(Quantum meruit determines the amount to be paid for services when no contract exists or when there is doubt as to the amount due for the work performed but done under circumstances when payment could be expected. [http://dictionary.law. com])* Make sure you understand the term or have a legal professional explain it to you.

- **Do** make sure you have a **right to rescind clause**. The Federal Trade Commission has a **Cooling Off Rule** to protect consumers, giving them a three-day right of rescission to cancel a contract. But there are stipulations. For instance, this may only apply if you sign the contract in your home but not in the contractor's show-room. In most cases, this 3-day right to cancel may expire when the work begins or if you sign a document waiving your right to cancel. There may be other stipulations depending on the state you are in. Be sure to check with a trusted advisor or legal professional and have them explain your state's right to rescind laws. In most instances, this clause must legally be part of the contract.

- **Do** make sure you know exactly what your **exit/termination clause** is in your contract. Push come to shove, you need to know what your options are to terminate the contract. What happens if he doesn't show up for days or weeks or even as scheduled? What happens if the work is shoddy? What happens if the contractor becomes irate or threatening? What happens if the contractor doesn't return phone calls or emails? How long should you give him to return to the project after disappearing before you can terminate the contract? If the contractor defaults on the contract, are you entitled to any money? The contractor may have a clause in the contract that if you terminate early for any reason, you still have to give him a percentage of the project cost. You need to be protected as well. Be sure to consult with an attorney or trusted advisor if you need help with the proper wording.

- **Do** add to your contract a **conflict resolution clause**. In other words, how do the two of you resolve a dispute? Most contractors want you to agree to mediation and/or arbitration and they usually have this clause in their contract. Look for that clause and read it. Arbitration may mean you lose your right to a court hearing or lawsuit. This is very important to understand or have an attorney advise you on. Maybe you and the contractor can agree to abide by the decision of a third-party code certified inspector. If so, make sure you both agree to an inspector, and how he is to be paid, before the project begins and include that inspector's information in your contract. Keep in mind, some states and local municipalities require inspectors to be licensed.

- **Do** try to add a clause in the contract where the contractor waives any workman's liens in the event of a dispute. Here's another instance where an attorney could really be of value before you sign anything.

- **Do** add to your contract a **Notice of Default** clause explaining how you will notify the contractor of any default. Maybe you will send any notices to the contractor by certified mail and give him 7 days after receipt to fix the problem before you seek legal recourse. Your attorney can help you with this clause.

- **Do** consider adding a **penalty clause** for **liquidated damages** to your contract. In other words, if the contractor does not finish by the end date, you can begin to withhold money (*i.e., $50-200 per day for every day over the project end date*). Keep in mind, most contractors will not want to include this in the contract. This is where a construction attorney is an excellent advisor. This may keep the contractor from starting your job then disappearing for days or weeks. Keep in mind, if it is raining, the contractor may not be able to work on the roof that day, so you have to forgive that day. This is why the daily project journal is so important (*described later*).

  > **Note:** If your attorney recommends a **penalty clause** in your contract, <u>be sure to state in the contract that the penalty (money) will be deducted from payments owed the contractor</u>. Otherwise, you may have to pay the contractor in full and then try to collect the penalty from him later. Your attorney will know what is applicable in your state. If a contractor has a problem with the penalty clause, you can agree to extend the contract *"end"*

date allowing him time to complete the job, but you really should have a penalty clause in your contract. Experienced contractors know how long a job should take.

- **Do** state in the contract that the contractor is responsible for getting signed lien releases from the suppliers and all subcontractors before you make any payments.

- **Do** include a *"time is of the essence"* clause in your contract. This is a clause that means failure to complete the job in a timely manner can be considered a breach of contract. This is why it is important to have an *end* date in your contract.

- **Do** ask your attorney about the **Statute of Repose** specific to your state. This is a law that prohibits you from claims for construction defects beyond a specific time after the contractor has finished your job.

- **Do** consider adding a clause in the contract that if the work is completed ahead of schedule, you agree to pay a little more (*state how much more*). This should encourage the contractor to focus on getting your job done.

DON'Ts

- **Don't** let a contractor scare you into a hasty decision to sign a contract or pay for work upfront. If you feel you are in an urgent situation, tell your contractor you never do anything without discussing it with your insurance agent and/or attorney first.

- **Don't** allow anyone to pressure you into signing any document that is incomplete, vague, or that you don't understand.

- **Don't** sign a contract that does not include a project beginning and <u>ending</u> date. (*We've seen many contracts with no end date.*) This is important when the contractor doesn't finish the job on time but asks to be paid for overtime. If they didn't show up for two days, even though the weather was fine, then he should not be paid overtime. Don't forget to put it in writing (*keep a copy of your note denying overtime pay*), and enter all pertinent information in your daily progress journal (*discussed later*).

- **Don't** ever sign a contract that has blank spaces. Blank spaces allow a dishonest contractor to make changes in the document by fraudulently adding information or modifying details after you've signed it. A contract with blank spaces is always a no-no. All blank spaces must be filled in or marked through (*i.e., N/A, not applicable, XXX, etc.*).

- **Don't** sign a contract that does not list the exact brands, grades, sizes, serial numbers, manufacturers, colors, etc. of all materials/appliances to be used. This can be detailed in the quote or Scope of Work and should be attached to the contract.

- **Don't** allow the contractor to walk off with the contract without you having a copy of what you signed. If you don't have a copy, you cannot prove you did not agree to any alterations he makes. If you don't have a copy machine nearby or the contract does not have a *carbon* copy, don't sign anything. Wait until you both are able to get a copy immediately after signing.

- **Don't** sign any contract where the contractor implies the contract cannot be canceled.

- **Don't** sign any contract that has an indemnity clause or hold harmless clause that only protects the contractor. Most form contracts that he gives you will protect him from any liability. At the least, the contract should protect you too. Many times, both parties will agree to the person at fault having liability, but this must be included in your contract. Here is where a construction attorney is extremely valuable.

- **Don't** forget to specify in the contract other issues such as work-day restrictions, smoking areas, removal and replacement of property, weather delays, punch list, lunch breaks, parking, etc.

Mediation/Arbitration

Mediation or Arbitration? Many consumers confuse mediation and arbitration. They are similar remedial procedures, but here is how they are different: **Mediation** is customarily a neutral third party, non-binding negotiation for the parties to come to a mutually agreed resolution of a dispute. **Arbitration**, on the other hand, is more like a court imposed decision; arbitrators act more like judges and make decisions based on evidence and legal precedents. Their decision is usually binding and final, but may not be so in all jurisdictions. Your attorney will know.

Many homeowners told us that when they agreed to go with binding arbitration they didn't realize that it took away their rights to go to court.

Many contractors prefer arbitration and may have an arbitration clause in their contract. You do not have to sign any agreement obligating you to arbitration. Have your attorney review your contract to be sure you are protected.

Are these things in your contract?

☑ CHECKLIST: Contract	Check Off
Complete legal name of the contractor?	
Complete legal name of the contractor's company?	
If applicable, contractor's license number?	
Contractor's business license number?	
Contractor's contact information (*physical address, not post office*) and phone number, cell, fax, email address, etc.?	
The contractor's insurance information? (*dates of coverage, policy limits, etc.*)	
Your name and address of the property being repair or remodeled?	
Does the contract have a start date?	
Does the contract have an end date?	
Does the contract have a clause that the contract is only applicable if financing (*insurance company or financial institution*) is obtained?	
Does the contract list the names, license numbers, contact information and insurance coverage of everyone who will be working in your home or on your property?	
The full Scope of Work – Does the contract include total breakdown of labor, equipment, exact materials/ supplies, cost, finance charges, taxes and fees, etc.?	

Have you added "Plan B" materials into the contract in case the materials/ supplies you requested are not available (*discontinued, out of stock, etc.*)?	
Is the contract a fixed contract?	
Who will be responsible for obtaining all building and other permits required, and any and all inspections? Does the contract state you are to receive copies of all permits and inspection results?	
Does the contract detail that the contractor is responsible for any damage he causes?	
Does the contract address who is responsible if the subcontractors don't do their work correctly?	
Does the contract state that the contractor will be responsible for meeting all workplace health and safety regulations?	
Does the contract the state that payments will cease until any code violations are corrected?	
Does the contract (*or the Scope of Work attached to the contract*) detail info about any large equipment to be used on your property?	
Is there a notice of default clause?	
Does the contract state who will be on the property doing what, on what days? Who will be the on-site supervisor?	

Does the contract identify who will be responsible for any utility issues, i.e., avoiding underground power lines, utility issues, gas lines, etc.? (*discussed later*)	
Does the contract state instructions for any surveys, engineering, plans, soil issues, etc.?	
Are there indemnity clauses (*sometimes referred to as "hold harmless"*) in your contract? If so, do they protect you as well as the contractor?	
Does the contract state that the contractor will perform the job to the standards (*or higher*) of the building codes of your jurisdiction?	
Is the payment schedule detailed in the contract? (*Payments should be made based on progress of work completed, not based on time.*) Does the contract include when payments will be made (*such as after the work is done and inspections are approved, after lien releases/waivers received, etc.*)?	
Is it detailed in your contract when you are allowed to withhold money from the contractor (*i.e., when he doesn't show up, when he performs shoddy construction, etc.*)? *This is where an attorney can come in handy to protect you from having to pay a contractor when he isn't living up to his end of the bargain.*	

Is there a penalty clause included if the completion date (*after legitimate extensions/delays*) is not met? Does this clause outline liquidated damages?	
Is there a termination/exit clause? (*What happens if the contractor does not start or complete the work? What happens if he only shows up every three weeks? You need a way to get out of the contract if the contractor is not professional. This is a good time to consult an attorney or trusted advisor.*)	
Is there a conflict resolution clause? (*What you and the contractor agree to if there is a problem. Contractors like for this to be mediation and/or arbitration. But that doesn't always work in your favor. This is a good time to consult an attorney or trusted advisor.*)	
Procedure for change orders: (*Your contract should have information that states how change orders will be handled. Just be sure to indicate that they must always be in writing, signed off on by both you and the contractor, and added as an addendum to your original contract.*)	
Does the contract address lien release/lien waiver requirements? (*This is so important.*)	
Does your contract include a guarantee or warranty on materials and workmanship?	
Does the contract include a "***time is of the essence***" clause?	

Does the contract include a *"3 day right of refusal"* clause?	
Does the contract address workday restrictions, smoking on site, hours of work, lunch breaks, where workers will park, etc.?	
Does the contract include who is responsible for clean up (punch list)?	
Does your contract have a *retainage clause (you will withhold final payment until punch list items are completed, property is cleaned up, debris removed from the property, lien releases/waivers received, warranties received, manuals received, etc.)? Another great reason to seek the advice of a legal professional in your state.*	
Does the contract state that if the contractor completes the work ahead of schedule, you agree to pay a little more? *(this is not mandatory)*	

We realize we sound like a broken record; however, we cannot stress enough how important it is to consult an attorney or trusted legal advisor before you sign anything you don't fully understand.

Now your contract has been signed and you are ready for the contractor to begin work based on the start date you both agreed to. But there are just a few more things you need to do first.

Preparing for the Contractor to Begin Working

Before the contractor begins any work, take as many good, clear pictures as you can. If you need to determine the size of something in the picture, you can always put a ruler, quarter, or some other measurable object next to it so you have an accurate reading of the size.

Taking pictures before the project begins is very important, especially if there are any issues or problems with the contractor's work down the road.

Safety Concerns Before the Contractor Begins

Here are a few things to think about before you allow the contractor into your home to begin working.

Your contractor should call your utility company(ies), *before* any digging is done on your property to make sure they don't hit or damage underground utilities. This is very important. This information can be found at **www.call811.com**. Also, be sure to mark the location of your sprinkler system or garden/plant areas so they are not damaged.

Decide where contractors can park, where they will eat their lunch, where they will put their trash and where they will go to the bathroom. If they are going to be there for quite a while, a portable toilet may be a good idea!

Don't give the contractor keys to your house and/or the alarm code. There should be no reason for the contractor to have them if you are at home. If you are away from home and he needs access, change the locks when the job is complete and give him a temporary alarm code.

Don't allow children to be unattended when contractors or subcontractors are in the house. Not only as a measure to protect them from people you don't really know, but also to keep them from wandering into or playing in work areas and getting hurt. Remove your pets during construction so that they are not terrified by construction noises or hurt by construction materials.

Put away all your valuables. That means any jewelry, paperwork you have lying around with your social security number on it, bank statements, laptops, cell phones, anything you do not want to lose.

While most contractors are honest, there is no need to take any chances.

Be sure to remove anything that can be easily broken, even if you don't consider it a valuable.

Here are a few last minute items you need to determine before the contractor begins.

CHECKLIST: Last Minute Details	Yes/No
Have you put away all your valuables? Breakables?	
Have you made arrangements for your children? Pets?	
Have your underground utilities and/or landscaping been marked?	
Have you designated parking, bathroom facilities, etc. for the workers?	
Do you have a copy of all necessary permits?	

CHAPTER 6

During the Project

As your project gets underway, it's also time to take more steps to protect yourself. We call it: DOCUMENTATION! DOCUMENTATION! DOCUMENTATION! You can use the forms we've provided below or create your own. It is important to track your progress by documenting everything and taking many good, clear pictures.

You should already have some "before" pictures of your project before any work begins. Photos are great documentation and should be done daily or at least every other day. And be sure the contractor sees you doing it. This will let him know that you are very involved in keeping track of the work being done. This should encourage him to focus on getting things right. When he notices that you're paying close attention, he will realize he has less of an opportunity to take advantage of you. Photos also come in handy later on down the road if you need to remember what may be behind your drywall.

You hired the general contractor to manage all aspects of your project, including subcontractors, work crews, material and equipment suppliers, building inspectors, and all the processes to complete your project. However, you should "oversee" your general contractor. Talk to him throughout the project, if possible, at the end of each day.

This will cut down on any miscommunication between you and the contractor, which is a big problem in the industry.

Do ask questions, but without being a bother. That means, feel free to ask all the questions you want, but not so many that the contractor is distracted from the project. The majority of your questions should have been asked before the project began. However, as you monitor the contractor's work, if something appears odd, you should ask questions or voice your concerns.

Sometimes homeowners are afraid to approach the contractor if the work appears to be shoddy or substandard. Remember, it's your home and your money. The contractor works for you. You're the boss. Ask questions. You can always have a family member, friend or neighbor come inspect the issue and speak to the contractor with you.

Know who will be in your home on each day and what they are expected to do while they are on your property. Then, after the crew leaves each day, closely check all work areas and make sure all entryways (*doors, windows, garages*) are locked and secured. We've heard stories of workers unlocking windows with the intent of robbing the homeowner later.

Remember to keep a file folder of all documents associated with your project.

Daily Progress Journal

Keep a daily progress journal and document all conversations and activities. Other things you should include in each day's entry are: daily weather conditions, what materials were delivered and/or installed, what major tools and equipment were used that day, who showed up for work, etc. For reference, your journal entries could look like the example below:

Daily Journal

Date	Who is on the Property	Daily Details
March 15	Contractor Electrician	Contractor and electrician showed up at 9am. Electrician installed wiring in the basement. Contractor put tile floor down in the kitchen. The jobs look good to me. They finished at 4:30pm. Contractor said they will be back tomorrow to repair the roof.
March 16	No One	No one showed up today. It was sunny and 75 degrees.
March 17	No One	No one showed up. It rained all day. Called the contractor and left a message on his voice mail that I wanted to know when they were coming back to complete the remaining work.
March 18	No One	No one showed up. No rain expected today although it's cloudy. Left another message for the contractor to contact me regarding completing the work. Did not hear back from him.
March 19	Contractor Plumber	Contractor and plumber showed up. Contractor said pipes under the sink are bad and will have to be replaced. Contractor presented me with a change order. I had an inspector confirm the problem. I signed the change order and made it a part of the contract.

Your daily progress journal should also detail any problems you are having with the contractor, the quality of the work, etc. It should indicate when you advised the contractor of these problems, including when you advised him in writing (*which you should always do, so you have a paper trail*). This information will come in handy if you ever need to terminate your contract and the contractor takes you to court. Be sure to take pictures of any shoddy workmanship.

You can never have too much documentation so write down as much as you want.

Daily Journal

Date	Who is on the Property	Daily Details

Change Orders

Once the project gets going, changes happen. They can be changes suggested by the contractor or by you. Maybe after the contractor opened up a wall, he discovered faulty pipes. Or you, the homeowner, don't like the navy blue paint you chose and now you want to change it to aqua blue. Regardless, all changes should be made in writing and signed off on by you and the contractor.

Change orders almost always change the bottom line cost. Be sure you are okay with that cost before you sign any change orders. You should also include the time it will take to complete the change. Does it change the *end* date in your contract?

Let's talk about where a lot of homeowners get into trouble. The contractor agrees to do something *"off the record"* for a discounted price or just out of the goodness of his heart. Homeowners think this is a great thing; oftentimes it is not. Sometimes, what the contractor is adding or changing may void your manufacturer's warranty. Sometimes, it may cause other problems. Maybe he offers to add an extra light to the light track, but the light track cannot handle another light. When a problem occurs because of that *"extra"* thing, having an agreement in writing gives you enforcement rights.

Remember, change orders can be expensive, especially if you yourself initiate the change. Good careful planning ahead of time helps keep change orders to a minimum, to keep costs from rising. Be sure of the exact color of paint before the contractor paints your walls. Make sure you want mahogany on your floors instead of bamboo.

Sometimes, a contractor will start a job, get really into it, and then tell you they found unexpected problems and they are going to need more money. Now that he has your home in a mess, you feel obligated to pay him whatever he asks for. This is where you may need to get a second opinion if you have questions or concerns.

You can always hire an inspector, engineer, etc. (*depending on the problem*) to confirm or negate what the contractor is telling you.

Sometimes, the contractor may do something wrong and a change order may be necessary. If he does something wrong, he should fix it at his expense.

Note: Sometimes, after an inspection, the city/county may require additional work to bring something up to code (*code compliance*). This too, should be done in the form of a change order and signed by you and the contractor. And more often than not, the contractor should pay for this because he is supposed to know code requirements before he begins the work. Make sure it is defined in your contract.

If Things Go Wrong – Conflict Resolution

Chances are, at some point in the project, you and the contractor may be at such odds that you cannot stand to be in the same room with each other. This is normal. However, there are ways to amicably resolve any conflicts. First, talk to the contractor and see if the two of you can come to an agreement on how to handle the problem. Once your contractor agrees to resolve the issue, write a letter to him outlining what you both agreed to and the timeframe in which it is to be done, and have him confirm his agreement in writing (*signature*).

You might consider having an independent code certified inspector take a look at the problem and render a decision you both agree to. Make sure you have added that inspector's name to your contract before any work begins. Because, by the time there is a dispute, you don't want to use any inspector he chooses and vice versa. Also include who is responsible for paying him. The extra money to pay the inspector may be worth your peace of mind.

This is where documentation is so important. Remember to enter everything about the situation in the daily progress journal/notes you are keeping. If the problem isn't resolved to your satisfaction, then look at your contract to determine what your options are, or call your attorney.

Be sure to take pictures of the problem and keep them in your file. Digital photos are inexpensive, so take as many pictures as necessary to be sure they *"show"* the issue. Include a ruler or other reference for size. Remember if these are to be used in a dispute, they need to show a judge or arbitrator the exact issue. Look at the pictures after taking them (*or better yet, have a friend who has not seen the problem, look at the photos to determine if they can "see" it too*).

It is always a good idea to send any official or contractually required correspondence to the contractor by certified mail, return receipt requested, so you can prove he received it. If you use email, request a receipt confirmation.

If he doesn't resolve the problem, send a second letter by certified mail, return receipt requested, asking for a resolution, explanation or meeting. If he still refuses, contact your attorney. And consider filing a complaint against him with your state contractor's board, licensing agency or Attorney General's office.

He probably won't, but if he threatens you verbally, call the police immediately and file a police report.

Other remedial options may be available to you under what's called **Unfair and Deceptive Practices (UDAP)** statutes which cover consumer rights to cancel a contract. Homeowners should check with a consumer protection attorney to determine what recourse is available to address deceptive and fraudulent residential construction.

Stay on him about taking responsibility for any problems that arise. And absolutely thank him when he does!

CHAPTER 7

After the Project

Now that you have gotten through the project and you are satisfied, you are ready to give the contractor his last payment and begin enjoying your new home repair or remodel. Wait. Not so fast! There are just a few last but important things you need to take care of.

Do you have written warranties for materials and all workmanship? In addition to warranties and instruction manuals, also keep track of materials used in the project. Make sure you have information on who manufactured, for instance, the roof shingles or the insulation. Keep these in your file folder. You will forget in a few months and these details will help you remember.

Have all inspections been approved? Keep in mind, the building inspector does not inspect paint colors and wallpaper, carpet, etc. Make sure you do a final inspection of your own.

If your project was large or expensive, you might consider hiring an independent **code certified inspector**, to inspect the work before you pay the contractor, to make sure everything has been done correctly. You can always hire an inspector to assess the project at various intervals while the work is in progress, not just at the end of the project. The choice is yours. But remember, the inspector cannot inspect what is behind the walls after the walls are added (*although* *photos may help*). While hiring an inspector may be an additional expense up front, it may be significantly less than having to re-do a project that was done incorrectly. Remember, construction mistakes can be costly, because mistakes frequently require demolition of work performed and then starting all over.

If you hired an architect at the beginning of your project, you may want written approval from your architect that the job was done right. While this may not always be necessary, it is something to consider.

Has your contractor given you a **final payment affidavit**? This is a document the contractor gives you that lists his name, company name, your name and address, how much you paid the contractor in full, and that all workers and suppliers have been paid. If any workers or suppliers have not been paid, they should be listed on the document. That way, you can make sure they are paid before you issue final payment to the contractor. No need to pay for something twice, if you can avoid it.

Certificate of Occupancy

Where applicable, you should be given a **Certificate of Occupancy** from your city/county. It signifies that all inspections have been done and approved and you can now occupy the building.

Notice of Completion

A **Notice of Completion** is basically a document that the contractor gives you indicating he has completed the project, if any inspections were necessary and if so, when they were done. It also indicates if any problems remain or if any inspections found issues. Sometimes a contractor will give you this, sometimes they won't. Just make sure you ask them to show, in writing, where inspections were done and what the results of the inspections were.

Certificate of Completion

After all work has been completed, you may be asked to sign a **Certificate of Completion** that certifies demolition, debris removal and clean up was done to your satisfaction. Any warranties you receive typically start on the date of the Certificate of Completion.

If the completion document says that you have verified that all work was done in accordance with any local code requirements, that may put you in a position of *"certifying"* something that you do not know (*unless you know the local building codes*). You may want to contact your local building department for information or a code certified inspector may be able to help.

Punch List

A **Punch List** is basically a list of things that still need to be done on your project. Here is a Punch List checklist. Make sure you have these items addressed before you issue final payment:

CHECKLIST: **Punch List**	**Check Off**
Has the job site been cleaned and cleared of materials, debris, tools, trash, cigarette butts, equipment, etc.?	
Has everything has been put back in its rightful place, paint touched up, walls cleaned, damage done by contractor/ workers repaired, etc?	
Do you have all written warranties/guarantees for materials and workmanship?	
Have all inspections been completed and approved? Do you have the documentation to confirm this?	
Has the contractor provided proof that all subcontractors and suppliers have been paid? Do you have all notarized lien waivers/releases?	

Does the work meet the standards spelled out in the contract?	
Does the work meet the standards of the manufacturer's installation requirements?	
If applicable, has the architect signed off on the work?	
Have you received a final payment affidavit from your contractor?	
Have you received a completion notification?	
If applicable, has a Notice of Completion been published in the appropriate local legal newspaper?	
Have you been presented a Certificate of Completion?	
Have you received a Certificate of Occupancy?	
Other	

Now you can give the contractor the final payment. Then thank them for their services, and begin enjoying the results!

What to Do if You Have Been Scammed

No one should ever feel foolish or irresponsible after being ripped-off. Cheaters spend hours and hours thinking of ways to deceive and swindle you, your neighbors, family members or friends. They have practiced their lines and quick answers. They know how to read your body language. There was a time when trust was part of how we did business, but many behaviors and practices have drastically changed.

If you are a victim of home repair fraud, please contact NCPHIF (**www.PreventContractorFraud.org**) so that we can direct you to the agency(ies) that can assist you. Only through reporting and tracking fraudulent activity can we help prevent dishonest contractors from victimizing others.

NCPHIF is an anti-fraud education and advocacy organization. We do not take part in attempts to collect or negotiate the return of monies from scam operators or dishonest contractors.

Be sure to contact your CPA or financial advisor and ask if you can write off your losses.

Fraud Recovery Funds

Some states have *Fraud Recovery Funds* that may allow restitution if you are financially damaged as a result of home repair fraud. However, it may require a lot of time and paperwork on your part, so be prepared.

The use of these funds may carry other restrictions and limitations specific to your state. Check with your local Consumer Protection Office or state licensing agency for information on these potential remedies. And do it quickly because there may be time limits or limited funds available. Also, there may be a ceiling on the award you may get. For instance, you may have lost $65,000 but the program may only award up to $15,000 per incident. It is a good idea to seek out this information before you begin a project so you are familiar with the process in the event anything goes wrong and you are victimized.

Project Checklist

Here is a quick list for you to make sure that you are, at least, getting the basics when dealing with a home repair contractor.

CHECKLIST: Project Checklist	Date Needed	Date Received/ Completed
BEFORE THE PROJECT		
Do you know exactly what home repair/rebuild/ remodel project you need or want done?		
Do you know what your budget is?		
Do you know how you are going to get the money for the project?		
Have you researched the project?		
Have you consulted with any architects or engineers?		
Have you gotten at least three estimates from contractors?		
Do these contractors specialize in the work you need to have done?		
Have you selected the contractors you are interested in using?		
Have you gotten at least three quotes from the contractors you are interested in using?		
Have you done background checks on each contractor?		
Have you gotten references on each contractor?		
Have you verified the contractor's insurance coverage?		
Have you verified that the contractor's "*business*" license is active and compliant?		
Have you verified that the contractor's "*contractor's*" license is active and compliant, where applicable?		

Question		
Have you verified the contractor is bonded, if applicable?		
Have you selected the contractor you are going to use?		
Have you considered purchasing a performance/completion bond, payment bond, etc?		
Have you met with the contractor to get the names and background information of all subcontractors?		
Have you met with the contractor to determine exactly what will be done (*Scope of Work*)?		
Have you and the contractor agreed to a payment schedule?		
Have you thoroughly reviewed and understand the contract?		
Has your attorney reviewed the contract and advised you on it?		
Have you taken pictures before any work begins?		
Have you secured your valuables?		
Do you have copies of all permits?		
DURING THE PROJECT		
Have you started a daily progress journal?		
Are you taking pictures throughout the project?		
Are you getting a daily update of the progress from the contractor?		
Are you getting all change orders in writing?		

AFTER THE PROJECT		
Has the project been completed?		
Has the property been cleared and cleaned of all debris, materials, equipment, etc.?		
Have all inspections been approved?		
Have all lien waivers/releases been notarized and signed?		
Do you have a final payment affidavit signed by the contractor and notarized?		
Do you have all your papers, i.e., warranties, etc.		
Do you have all applicable notices? Notice of Completion? Certificate of Occupancy? Etc.		

CHAPTER 8

Disasters

Disaster Victims are a Big Target for Home Repair Scams

With so many large and frequent weather related disasters happening, we wanted to dedicate a special section for disaster victims.

A tornado, hurricane or flood sweeps through your city and destroys hundreds of homes. When it finally passes over, debris is everywhere. Homes and properties as far as you can see are damaged and many are completely destroyed. Power lines are down; there is a smell of gas in the air; you cannot tell where streets meet sidewalks. People are walking around traumatized by the *train-like* sound, darkness, destruction, and/or what they believe was the most fearful wind/water in the world. Yet, there are swarms of contractors already on the scene. You wonder, *"How the heck did they get here so quickly?"* Answer: they monitor climate alerts where devastation is predicted to happen.

After a disaster, it's easy to assume everyone who approaches you is compassionate and trustworthy. The idea of being deceived does not cross your mind at this vulnerable time. Your guard is down. Many times, disaster victims are too traumatized to think clearly or rationally about hiring contractors. Taking advantage of people under these circumstances is unthinkable, but predators arrive in droves, intent on doing just that. Because of the severe emotional stress on a disaster victim, it is very easy for them to make an illogical decision.

Here are some preventative steps NCPHIF urges disaster victims to take:

In a Hurry To Get Back to Normal

Once you have been given the clearance by law enforcement to assess your damage after a disaster, only do what is absolutely necessary to avoid further damage. This usually includes things like putting a tarp on your damaged roof, boarding up broken windows, etc. Then, you have plenty of time to find a reputable contractor. Keep in mind - because of all the damage and destruction, it may take a while to get a legitimate contractor to do your repairs.

One of the biggest problems disaster victims face is dishonest contractors taking advantage of their vulnerability. Disaster victims want to get beyond the traumatic experience by getting back to normal as quickly as possible. Many times, this stress causes them to make illogical decisions when it comes to hiring contractors. We have had many homeowners who, two years after a disaster, are still having problems with the contractor and are still not back in their homes.

After a disaster, materials are in short supply, and so is legitimate labor. This is when you become the most vulnerable to a scammer who says all the things you want to hear and before you know it, you have given him 50 percent of your money up front to get on his immediate schedule and signed a contract you didn't even read. Then he disappears. Now you don't have the money to replace what was taken so you end up foreclosing on the home you raised your children in, grew up in, or worked so hard to acquire. You've now been victimized twice, once by the disaster and now by a shady contractor. This can be avoided. Read on.

Screening Contractors

After disasters, many contractors are on the scene trying to get your business and lock you into a contract. There are storm restoration contractors, public adjusters, roofers, plumbers, electricians, debris removers, tree removal services, etc. who will all be vying for your business. While they are *disaster* experts, you still need to screen them like you would any other workers on your property.

Some disaster contractors (*storm restoration specialists, roofers, etc.*) may tell you they know insurance inside and out. The question is: are they licensed by the state? If they are not licensed as insurance specialists by the state, you should be concerned. Always call your state's insurance department to confirm any insurance licensing requirements. This type of licensing protects you, by requiring anyone who claims to be an insurance representative to maintain education requirements, code of ethics and other professional standards. When it comes to insurance representation, only deal with those who are licensed by the state, period.

After disasters, cities/counties may set up special requirements for any contractors seeking disaster repair work. Be sure to contact your city/county to find out what they have set up to help protect you from shady contractors.

Note: Fire or flood damage requires a professional contractor experienced in that line of work. Don't hire your plumber, painter, etc. to oversee your fire damage repair just because he said he can *"cut you a deal."*

Asking for ID

One way to protect yourself immediately is to ask for identification from anyone who approaches you and tells you they are a contractor, government official, nonprofit agency representative, volunteer, or holds some other official capacity. Ask for an ID even if they are dressed in clothes that look official. If anyone asks you for money or a fee for service of any kind, they are not legitimate! We are not aware of ANY situation where any agency would ask for money after a disaster.

Check with your local police department if you have any questions.

Preventing Theft of Items On Your Property

After a disaster, thieves come into the area to steal metal, copper and other items from damaged properties as well as search for your valuables lost in the debris. Unfortunately, there are people who will use tragic circumstances as a means of taking advantage of you and others. More and more, local law enforcement is stepping up to protect the property of disaster victims by closing off damaged areas and requiring proper credentials from anyone trying to enter the area. But sometimes, that's just not enough.

After a disaster, your papers and personal belongings may be destroyed or scattered miles away from your home. Still, look around your immediate surroundings and gather up any items that may reveal your private information, including computer drives and other electronic devices with memory chips. Identity fraud is another rip-off rampant in our nation; we don't want you victimized by yet another form of fraud. Before a disaster is a good time to ask your insurance agent about any identity theft coverage and what happens in the event of theft of your personal belongings. Discuss with your insurance agent the possibility of identity theft insurance coverage for some period after a disaster as well. You can also "freeze" your credit file to protect yourself.

> **NCPHIF TIP:** As a preventative measure, you should already have an inventory of everything of value in your home. Take pictures and write a clear and detailed description of each item. For example, include dates of purchase, serial numbers, model

numbers, color, amount paid for the item, receipts, and any other information that will help you file a claim to cover your losses if a disaster happens. Some people use a video camera. Keep a copy of your inventory list stored away from your home, in free online storage or maybe with a trusted family member in another city. Most insurance companies have a brochure detailing what should be done in advance and even provide inventory checklists that you can use. Be sure to get one from your insurance agent and update it frequently.

Every homeowner should give some thought as to what types of disasters are possible where he or she lives, then create a plan. Your plan should include family communications, emergency kits, your insurance information and contacts. Have a copy of this book in your disaster kit also. When you experience a disaster first hand, you may be overwhelmed. This is when instructions that are already in place can be incredibly helpful. You will be glad you already have a plan in place, to fall back on.

Note: It is a good idea to find and screen a contractor before you need one.

Expertise is Important

Make sure you use a contractor who is an expert at the job you need done. For instance, don't hire a plumber to repair your roof or a cabinet installer to repair your cracked swimming pool. Ask the contractor what his specialty is before you tell him what you need done. If you tell him you need a new garage door installed, he may tell you that is what his specialty is, even though he is a plumber. Now, sometimes, contractors are experts at more than one type of service. But you will find this out when you ask him what his specialty is.

Filing an Insurance Claim

First, call your insurance agent and alert them to your situation (*keeping in mind your local insurance agent may also be a victim of the disaster and may not return your call right away*). Your agent usually has the authority to issue funds for you to handle any immediate emergencies. Just be sure to keep all receipts. Determine what emergency repairs are needed and what can wait.

After a disaster, insurance companies dispatch disaster response teams to the area so there may not be a need to wait for a response from your personal insurance agent. During catastrophes, insurance companies often use independent adjusters simply because they may not have enough staff to cover the volume, so don't be alarmed if your carrier sends someone other than an employee. When the adjuster comes to your property, verify their credentials. If the adjuster asks you for any money, inform your insurance company right away. Claim adjusters are paid by the insurance company, and they do not "*collect*" deductibles.

When you speak with your insurance agent or company, keep a record of the date, time, person you spoke with, their contact number or email address, what you discussed, and what the next steps will be. In disasters, many times, insurance agents and companies are overwhelmed in handling all of their customers. Having this information at all times may help them handle your claim much faster.

You may also want to contact your mortgage lender and let them know you have damage.

Mold Specialists

After a hurricane or flood, water entering your home can lead to major mold problems. It is always a good idea to hire a mold expert to determine if there is moisture in your home, especially where you cannot see it, such as behind your walls. But beware, there are a lot of con artists in the mold remediation business.

> **Note:** If someone tells you they are a "certified mold inspector" be sure to ask them who they were certified by and then investigate to see what the requirements are to become certified. Did they just take a course on line and then pay a fee for certification? Did they take in-class training? Were they tested? Did they do any on-the-job training? How many years have they been in business? Screen them like you would any other contractor.

"Storm Chasers" and Other Out of Town Contractors

Many out-of-town and out-of-state contractors will head your way after a disaster. Some good. Some bad. They are sometimes referred to as *travelers, gypsies, storm chasers*, etc. They will go door-to-door seeking jobs. If at all possible, you should use a local contractor. However, after a large disaster, your community may not have enough local contractors available to do the work. After all, many of them may also be victims of the same disaster. Because you want to get back to normal as soon as you can, you may consider hiring an out-of-town or out-of-state contractor. If you hire one, you should consider the likelihood of them coming all the way back to your home to fix whatever may go wrong with their work. And, if the contractor is from another state, before they work on your home, be sure that they are qualified to do business in your state. They may not be in compliance with or even be aware of your particular state's laws and ordinances, which may make you responsible for any noncompliance issues that may come up. If you have to sue an out-of-state contractor, you may have to go to their state to collect any judgment (*and there is no guarantee you'll get it*).

These are just a few things to be aware of in the event of a storm/disaster and your home is damaged or destroyed. You can usually find NCPHIF on-site in disaster areas, assisting disaster victims with their rebuild process. NCPHIF is always available (**www.PreventContractorFraud.org**) to answer any questions disaster victims have about dealing with contractors during their rebuild process.

CHAPTER 9

Are You Smarter than a Dishonest Contractor?

Common and Not So Common Scams

Day in and day out, NCPHIF is contacted by consumers who have been scammed. This section identifies the victim, the scam, and tips to help you avoid becoming the next victim. Keep in mind, these recommendations are not legal advice, but only information, to help protect you and your most valuable asset—your home. The information presented here is not 100 percent characteristic of every scam being committed, but it alerts you to a number of risks and rip-off tactics most often used by bad actors operating under the guise of trustworthy home repair contractors. Often the most common scams have variations so beware.

Victims, Scams and NCPHIF Tips

Here are some victims and scams we want to make you aware of and some NCPHIF tips to protect yourself.

SCAM ALERT!

THE VICTIM: A homeowner who thinks they are smarter than a dishonest contractor.

THE SCAM: An attorney hired a contractor to install a pool. Feeling savvy enough to deal with the pool contractor, she told him he was not getting any money up front. This did not appear to be a problem. He began work on the project, dug an enormous hole in the woman's backyard, after which he requested $21,000 to purchase all the materials and supplies to complete the installation. Seeing that he took the time to dig the hole, the attorney gave the money to the contractor. She never saw him again!

NCPHIF TIP: Rip-offs and scams happen to people from all walks of life. Dishonest contractors know how to take advantage of people who think they are too smart, too savvy, or too educated to be victimized. We have met fraud victims who are doctors, lawyers, celebrities, wealth managers -- even mayors, police chiefs and detectives -- who have been scammed by shady contractors. Absolutely no homeowner is immune! Some may not be "*as*" vulnerable, but certainly all are potential victims.

SCAM ALERT!

THE VICTIM: A homeowner who believes a contractor when he says he is *"licensed and insured"* or *"licensed and bonded"*.

THE SCAM: A first-time homebuyer hires a contractor because he told her he was *"licensed and insured"* so she took that to mean he held the required **contractor's license** (*in this case, a plumber's license*). After he performed shoddy construction in her bathroom, she discovered that he only had a **business license**.

> **NCPHIF TIP:** A **business license** and a **contractor's license** are two totally separate things (*discussed in this book*). Many states require contractors to have a **contractor's license**, although some states do not require one for every construction related task. If one is required, make sure you get a copy of it and verify it with your state licensing agency. Often this can be done online.
>
> Many residential contractors are not *bonded* or *insured* as often claimed. As a homeowner, do NOT take a contractor's word when he tells you he is licensed, bonded and/ or insured. Verify the information with the appropriate company or agency.

SCAM ALERT!

THE VICTIM: A homeowner who picks a contractor because his bid is lower than all the other bids.

THE SCAM: Two contractors quoted $9,000 and $9,500. A third quoted $3,000. The homeowner chose the lower estimate of $3,000. She discovered that instead of putting pipes under her bathroom sink, he used garden hoses. By the time she discovered the major water damage, the service provider was long gone.

NCPHIF TIP: Think twice about hiring a contractor based solely on a low bid. Many times, lower quotes are another tactic used by scammers just to get the job. Once he has his foot in your door, to live up to that low price offer, he may diminish the quality of service by cutting corners somewhere else in your project. Or he may *"create"* other problems and tell you he *"discovered"* them which may end up costing you more than the original quote.

SCAM ALERT!

THE VICTIM: A homeowner who meets with a salesperson and not the contractor.

THE SCAM: A senior met with a salesperson and signed a contract without knowing who the contractor was. The contractor was a roofer who had scammed several others in another state. He hired the salesperson to find him work.

NCPHIF TIP: Tell the salesperson thank you and decline to do business with anyone who won't introduce themselves. You have a right to know who will be coming on your property or in your home before you sign any contract.

SCAM ALERT!

THE VICTIM: A homeowner who believes the contractor when he says they don't need a building permit.

THE SCAM: A contractor told a homeowner they did not need a building permit. However, the work did, in fact, require a permit. A neighbor noticed there was no permit notice posted and called the city to report it. Because the homeowner did not have a permit and the work failed to meet code, the city made the homeowner tear down the construction to the foundation.

> **NCPHIF TIP:** Many permit requirements are posted online by local jurisdictions. You can always call your local building department to confirm whether or not a building permit is required for any or all of the work you need done. Many times, unlicensed contractors will try to scam you because they must have proper licensing to pull a permit. Also, you can have a contractor put it in writing if a building permit is not required.

SCAM ALERT!

THE VICTIM: A homeowner who has to pay the contractor when he terminates the contract.

THE SCAM: A contractor was not doing the job as expected, would not show up and would not return the homeowner's telephone calls. The homeowner ended the relationship and refused to pay the contractor. The contractor demanded he be paid 20 percent of the project cost, as stated in the contract, because the homeowner terminated the agreement. The homeowner went to court to explain his side. The homeowner lost.

NCPHIF TIP: You absolutely must read and understand, thoroughly, any contract before you sign it. Be sure to have an exit/termination clause in your contract that protects you if the contractor doesn't show up, etc. This is where the expertise of an attorney is invaluable.

SCAM ALERT!

THE VICTIM: A homeowner who is promised a 100-year warranty.

THE SCAM: A homeowner hired a contractor based on the 100-year warranty. She thought that was a great level of security. If she was not happy with the work or if there were problems, the work was warranted. When the cabinets came loose from the wall six months later, the homeowner discovered the contractor went out of business and the warranty was invalid.

NCPHIF TIP: Remember, a labor warranty is only good as long as that contractor is in business and willing to honor the warranty.

SCAM ALERT!

THE VICTIM: A homeowner who tells a contractor how much money he has in his budget or how much the insurance company gave him.

THE SCAM: A homeowner told a contractor her budget was $50,000. When she got an estimate, it was $49,500. She attended our *SmartPower* workshop. Afterwards, she got two other estimates but did not reveal her budget: the quotes were $25,000 and $23,400.

NCPHIF TIP: Don't tell them your budget! If you reveal this information, the contractor may find ways to maximize your project's cost to your available money. If you tell him your budget is $80,000, how much do you think his estimate will be? How much money you have should have nothing to do with how much he charges to do the work. In some cases, when he asks what your budget is, he is trying to "qualify" you. We suggest you have a *wish list* of things you want to make it easier for him to give you a more accurate estimate.

SCAM ALERT!

THE VICTIM: A homeowner who gets a loan from a lender the contractor recommends.

THE SCAM: A woman secured funding for her roof repair through a finance company recommended by her contractor. The finance company gave the check directly to the contractor who then installed the new roof on top of the damaged roof. The next time it rained, the senior's roof leaked terribly. When her church member got up on the roof, he discovered that the work was extremely shoddy.

When the contractor didn't return her calls, she stopped making payments on the loan, hoping he would return to correct his sloppy work. That never happened. Meanwhile, the lender obtained a judgment against her for the repayment of the loan.

NCPHIF TIP: In many instances, beware of contractors who try to convince you to use their lender. This should be considered a possible conflict of interest. Consider your own bank or a local credit union. Always make sure you know exactly what your loan terms are, especially the interest rate and how the funds will be disbursed. Be careful borrowing money from finance companies you have never heard of.

SCAM ALERT!

THE VICTIM: A homeowner who thinks they are getting a deal from a contractor who offers them a discount on supplies/materials left over from another project.

THE SCAM: A contractor purchased extra supplies on the account of an unsuspecting homeowner. He then approached another homeowner and offered a 40 percent discount on those same supplies.

NCPHIF TIP: A good contractor typically estimates some waste (*about 10 percent*) on a project. Be wary of a contractor who has enough supplies left over to do another full job. They may have cut corners on the previous job or maybe they did a poor estimate. And if they overcharged or robbed the homeowner before you, what are *you* going to end up paying for to be used on a job after yours?

SCAM ALERT!

THE VICTIM: A homeowner who is told their prospective con-tractor is a spiritual/faith-based business (*he is a Christian, true believer, ordained by God to fix houses, etc.*).

THE SCAM: A homeowner was approached by a contractor who told him he was a "Born Again Christian" and his business was Christian-based. When the homeowner agreed to hire the contractor and gave him money up front, the contractor never returned.

> **NCPHIF TIP:** Scammers are now taking advantage of people by suggesting they are of the same faith in order to gain favor to do your project. Just because someone claims they are "*faith-based*" does not mean you should skip doing your due diligence (*background research*). NCPHIF has received many reports from victims who were scammed or defrauded by their pastors, deacons, relatives, neighbors, etc. Remember, your project is a business transaction. If the contractor is of the same faith, you can always invite them to your church. But for heaven's sake, don't let your guard down.

SCAM ALERT!

THE VICTIM: A homeowner who is offered a steep discount if they allow the contractor to use their home repair project as a "demo" for their neighbors to see.

THE SCAM: A contractor finished a homeowner's basement in a new subdivision. The job was done very well and at a steep discount since the homeowner agreed to tell her new neighbors about the contractor's work. Six of those neighbors liked the work and each gave the contractor a $6,000 deposit. The contractor took off with the money and never returned. The neighbors then assumed the homeowner was in on the scam.

NCPHIF TIP: Be careful. Many times, a *"demo"* can be a way for a dishonest contractor to get you, unknowingly, to help him with his scam. If *you* refer a contractor, always advise your neighbors to do their own background checks and caution them about giving money up front.

SCAM ALERT!

THE VICTIM: A homeowner who sued his contractor and won.

THE SCAM: A homeowner was awarded $50,000 by the courts after he sued a dishonest contractor. He was excited to have won. However, six years later, the homeowner only received $198 of the $50,000 he was expecting.

> **NCPHIF TIP:** Being proactive is key. It is crucial to check out the contractor as much as possible BEFORE you hire him. Getting a favorable judgment does not, by any means, guarantee that you will get reimbursed. You will have to continue to pursue the contractor to try to collect your money, all at your cost, and likely to no avail.

SCAM ALERT!

THE VICTIM: A homeowner who hires a contractor who just shows up at their door uninvited.

THE SCAM: A contractor shows up uninvited at the door of a homeowner. He tells the homeowner, *"...we're in the neighborhood today to offer you a 'special', 'discount' or 'free' deal on any work you need."*

> **NCPHIF TIP:** You should not use contractors who just show up at your door uninvited. You need time to perform your due diligence to see if they are a legitimate business. You should always find your own contractor. NCPHIF recommends finding and screening a contractor before you need one.

SCAM ALERT!

THE VICTIM: A homeowner who hires a contractor who comes to their door offering a free inspection.

THE SCAM: A pest control contractor came to a home and told the owner that he found *"this piece of wood on the side of their home"* which had heavy termite damage. He convinced the homeowner that they needed pest control treatment right away, and he had the deterrent on his truck. He said he could do the job at a discount if he could do it that day, while he was in the area. The wood was not from the homeowner's home and the "treatment" was water.

NCPHIF TIP: Some operators are known to intentionally *cause* damage during their inspection. Should you invite a contractor to inspect any part of your home, don't let them out of your sight. If the contractor finds something that needs to be done, let him see you take a picture of it so he understands that you will be very involved in any project. Tell him thank you but that you always get at least three estimates before you make any decisions. Don't feel rushed to hire anyone.

SCAM ALERT!

THE VICTIM: A homeowner who hires a contractor who is using another contractor's license number.

THE SCAM: A contractor is not licensed in your state so he uses the license number of a contractor who is. Sometimes with that contractor's knowledge (*they get paid*) and sometimes without that contractor's knowledge.

> **NCPHIF TIP:** Make sure that any contractor who works on your home has his own license number. Verify his license information with your state licensing board.
>
> And remember, what is the likelihood of him returning to fix any problems that come up after he has left town? If the contractor you used is from another state and he won't return to fix a problem, is the contractor with the actual license going to come and take care of the problem? Something to think about.

SCAM ALERT!

THE VICTIM: A homeowner who is offered a *discount* which is only good for the next hour or the next 24 hours.

THE SCAM: A senior agreed to a contractor's discount. He gave the contractor $800. The contractor said he was going to his truck to get the supplies, and drove off.

> **NCPHIF TIP:** Any sales representative or service provider offering a deal that is "good" for only one day or a few hours (**pressure selling**) is most likely trying to manipulate you or set you up for a scam. You should always have ample time to think about any offer, so don't be bullied into making a quick decision you may later regret. Legitimate contractors will always give you time to check them out. Remember, your rush to save may end up costing you more if you select the wrong contractor. (*An exception may be if a manufacturer offers a limited-time offer on a particular product and the offer is about to expire. In most cases this can be verified on the manufacturer's website.*)

SCAM ALERT!

THE VICTIM: A homeowner who is approached by a contractor who tries to scare them into believing that if they don't act right away, something terrible will happen.

THE SCAM: A contractor tells a homeowner that from the street he noticed that the house appears unstable on the left side and may collapse. He convinced the homeowner to allow him to contact their insurance company and file a claim, by offering to pay the homeowner's insurance deductible.

NCPHIF TIP: Don't let any contractor scare you into a hasty decision. Always be wary of sales people who try to scare you into signing for "urgent" repairs. If there is an insurance claim involved, tell your insurance agent what the contractor or salesperson is saying about the pressing need for getting your work done. If you are still unsure about how crucial your needs are, contact your local building department or a third party inspector. Many times, especially after a disaster, you may need emergency repairs, such as having your roof tarped (covered) or a portion of your home secured. You can have someone just do that emergency work, which will buy you time to find a good contractor to perform more permanent repairs.

SCAM ALERT!

THE VICTIM: A homeowner who is given a verbal quote by a contractor.

THE SCAM: A homeowner agreed to pay $3,000 for a job. Not taking the time to review the contract, he signs it. The contract stated the job would be $4,500. The homeowner told the contractor they agreed to $3,000 and he would not pay a penny more. The contractor filed a lien on the property.

> **NCPHIF TIP:** Always insist on a written contract and read it thoroughly to make sure that every detail of the job is included. Be sure to keep the original or at least a copy of the contract. If you are unsure about anything regarding your contract, we highly suggest asking a legal professional to review the contract before you sign.

SCAM ALERT!

THE VICTIM: A homeowner who signs what she thinks is a "waiver of liability" that allegedly protects her if the contractor gets hurt while doing an estimate.

THE SCAM: A roofer asked a homeowner to sign a document that authorized him to inspect her roof. He told her his insurance company required her authorization. She signed as requested. Afterwards, she was told that the document included a clause stating that if she did not use that particular roofing company for the job, she had to pay an "inspection fee" of $750 for the roofer's evaluation and write up of the damage to her roof.

NCPHIF TIP: Don't sign any document you do not read and understand. Don't take their oral explanation. Read it yourself. Contact your insurance agent or consult an attorney to help you grasp the scope and limits of any insurance waiver or any other contractual document.

SCAM ALERT!

THE VICTIM: A homeowner who hires a contractor who only takes cash.

THE SCAM: A young lady who only worked part-time for minimum wages hired a contractor to fix her heating unit. He told her he did not take credit cards or personal checks. She did not have any credit cards or a bank account so that seemed fair to her. She gave the contractor $200 cash to get supplies. She never saw him again.

NCPHIF TIP: This is another big red flag! Most legitimate contractors will accept a check or credit card. It is best to use a credit card, but if you must pay in cash, get an invoice that shows the name of the company, the contractor's name, the date, your property address, the amount that you paid, exactly what you are paying for, and the contractor's signature. Closely review the invoice and have it in your hand before you give the contractor your hard earned money!

Note: Before you hire a contractor, always ask what forms of payment he accepts.

SCAM ALERT!

THE VICTIM: A compassionate homeowner who falls prey to the contractor's sob story.

THE SCAM: A contractor told a homeowner that he had four children and his wife was ill and he needed money up front to get groceries. He further stated that he would go the extra mile to make sure the project was on time if the homeowner would comply. The homeowner gave the money to the contractor and never saw him again.

> **NCPHIF TIP:** Don't fall prey to a *"sob story"* pitch. The service provider's personal situation has nothing to do with the services you need. Don't develop an emotional relationship with the contractor. This is a business transaction. If an attempt to pull at your heartstrings is made, you can always help him find local nonprofits or community organizations that can service his personal needs. You should not advance your project money to resolve a contractor's personal problems.

SCAM ALERT!

THE VICTIM: A homeowner who allows work to start before they get a contract signed.

THE SCAM: A homeowner was told by a contractor, who happened to be in the neighborhood, that he could give the homeowner a steep discount of $500 for the sealant to seal his driveway. The homeowner agreed. Once completed, the contractor says the price did not include labor, which was $1,500.

> **NCPHIF TIP:** Never allow the contractor to start work before you outline in a contract, everything to be done and for what price. If the work is started before a contract is signed, the contractor can and may dramatically increase the price. Under most state law, if there is no written agreement and the contractor has improved your property, the contractor is entitled to be paid for time, materials and often profit and you are at risk of having a lien placed against your property for failure to pay. If the work is started without your permission, order the work to be stopped and if necessary, call the police.

> **Note:** Everything in writing!

SCAM ALERT!

THE VICTIM: A homeowner who is frightened or intimidated when they question the contractor about his poor workmanship, delay in responding, asking for more money, etc.

THE SCAM: A contractor did poor quality work. His attitude was menacing and intimidating, making the homeowner feel fearful about approaching him to discuss her concerns. She thought that reporting him to anyone, including the police, might bring more trouble to her.

> **NCPHIF TIP:** If you are female, it is always good to have another person present when you deal with a contractor so the contractor is aware that you are not as vulnerable as he may have assumed. If you ever feel threatened or frightened, contact your local police.

SCAM ALERT!

THE VICTIM: A homeowner who is asked for money up front by the contractor before he starts the project.

THE SCAM: After a tornado, a disaster victim was desperate to get back to normal as soon as possible. So he forked over 50 percent of the project cost, which the contractor required if the homeowner wanted his repairs done right away. He never saw the contractor again. He could not replace the money and he could not continue to pay rent on the temporary housing he secured and his mortgage at the same time. Since his home was too damaged to live in, he abandoned the property to foreclosure.

NCPHIF TIP: This is the biggest red flag of all! Some contractors will tell you they need money up front to pay for supplies and/or equipment. A number of consumer advisors suggest paying 10 percent of the project cost or $1,000, whichever is less, because, in fact, the contractor may need to purchase supplies. Some state laws regulate deposit amounts, some do not. In this book, we give you some options on how to handle the "money up front" issue.

SCAM ALERT!

THE VICTIM: A homeowner who gives money upfront to a contractor to purchase supplies.

THE SCAM: A homeowner gave a contractor $8,000 up front to purchase materials. The contractor performed a small portion of the job, and then disappeared with the money. Having lost $8,000, the homeowner now has to come up with another $8,000 to have someone else do the job. If he hires an attorney, that means additional monies to pay court costs and attorney's fees. Even if he wins in court, the homeowner may never recover his money. This is an unfortunate situation that can be easily avoided!

> **NCPHIF TIP:** Chances are the contractor is getting your supplies at a local store. Many times, you can meet him at the material supply store and pay for the supplies yourself. If he insists that he will get the supplies cheaper if he purchases them, you can always make your check out to the supplier. That way, he cannot take off with your money. And make sure you get a copy of all receipts.

SCAM ALERT!

THE VICTIM: A homeowner who doesn't stay with the contractor while he prepares an estimate.

THE SCAM: A homeowner had two guys knock on her door offering a *"free inspection"* for general work on her home. While one talked to her in the backyard about redoing her deck, the other slipped in the front door she just came out of and stole her jewelry and laptop.

> **NCPHIF TIP:** Make sure you follow any potential contractor around your home while they prepare an estimate. If more than one person shows up at your home, keep your eye on both of them. If you come out of your home, always lock the door behind you so no one can enter while you are not looking. Always be careful and be sure to avoid putting yourself in a vulnerable or dangerous position.

SCAM ALERT!

THE VICTIM: A homeowner who doesn't pay attention when a contractor unlocks a window.

THE SCAM: A homeowner, getting an estimate from a potential contractor, stepped away for a quick moment to grab her cell phone. Two days later, when she came home from work, she discovered her jewelry was gone. She called the police and it was determined that there was no evidence of forced entry. The contractor unlocked her window when she wasn't looking.

> **NCPHIF TIP:** Make sure you check all your windows/doors to make sure they are all locked after any prospective service provider leaves your property.

SCAM ALERT!

THE VICTIM: A homeowner who loves it when the contractor says he will pay their insurance deductible or that he will fill out their insurance paperwork for them.

THE SCAM: After convincing a homeowner that he was an expert at dealing with insurance companies and getting them to pay claims, a contractor filed an insurance claim on behalf of the homeowner. When the insurance company's adjuster came to do an inspection, it was determined that the claim was fraudulent. The insurance company canceled the homeowner's policy.

> **NCPHIF TIP:** Be very careful. Your insurance policy is between you and your insurance company. Any misrepresentation or outright fraudulent acts committed by the contractor may negatively affect you. For example, if you have a contractor who advises he will pay your insurance deductible, this may be prohibited by your state's regulatory agency or your insurer, so be very careful. Immediately contact your insurance agent for guidance because you may become a party to fraud and not even know it. Don't risk having your homeowner's policy canceled by your insurance company or being held accountable for a fraudulent claim. Remember, the motive for a contractor to collect on your insurance is to make a profit. He may ask you to sign falsified claim documents, and he does not care about the impact a false or fraudulent claim may have on you.

SCAM ALERT!

THE VICTIM: A homeowner who asks for the contractor's *certificate of insurance* but does not call the phone number on the certificate to verify coverage.

THE SCAM: An attorney smartly asked a contractor to show him his insurance card. Satisfied that the contractor had appropriate insurance coverage, he okayed the work to be done. When a day laborer fell off the roof, the homeowner discovered that the contractor had not paid his premium in over three months.

NCPHIF TIP: Call and verify that the contractor has an active policy for appropriate coverage with the insurance company listed on his insurance card. If you need help with this process, your personal insurance agent can help you verify that the contractor's policy is active and current, as well as the extent and appropriateness of coverage.

Note: Make sure that the contractor will have appropriate insurance coverage through the end of your project. For instance, if your project will take 3 months, make sure the contractor has coverage for the entire 3 months.

SCAM ALERT!

THE VICTIM: A homeowner who believes a salesperson or contractor who knocks on their door and tells them that there is hail damage to other homes in the neighborhood and they too, most likely need a new roof.

THE SCAM: A couple hired a roofer who came to their door and said that they had hail damage. The couple's neighbors hired the roofer so the couple agreed to hire him too. The couple gave him $7,000 to purchase materials and begin working to replace the roof. The contractor worked for two days and did not return. Then it rained. The weather damage inside the home required even more work and damaged their possessions, costing over $150,000.

NCPHIF TIP: Contact by uninvited service providers is always a red flag. You should always find your own contractor. If you are told you have hail damage, walk around your house and see if you have damage at ground level. Are there dents in your air conditioning unit or your car in the driveway? If not, then chances are you may not have roof damage. Never let anyone up on your roof without you being present because that individual can easily "create" damage.

SCAM ALERT!

THE VICTIM: A homeowner who sees a local phone number on the truck and assumes the contractor is local.

THE SCAM: The potential service provider has a local phone number listed on his truck, but his license plate is from another state. A homeowner hired a contractor he thought was local because of his local phone number. A few months later, when problems started, he called the number only to discover it was disconnected.

> **NCPHIF TIP:** Be very suspicious of contractors who list local telephone numbers but drive vehicles with out-of-state license plates. Chances are this contractor is from another state and obtained a local phone number to appear he is local. What are the chances of him returning if something goes wrong with the work he did on your home? If for any reason you decide to use this contractor, be sure to write down his license plate state and number, and take a picture of him; yes him, and his vehicle.

SCAM ALERT!

THE VICTIM: A homeowner who paid for upgraded materials, but the contractor installs lower quality, cheaper products.

THE SCAM: Unaware, a homeowner paid for a special grade of carpet, but a lower grade was installed. When the carpet started to unravel, the homeowner got his copy of the invoice and went to the retail supplier to complain. The supplier sent an inspector to the property to investigate. They discovered that the carpet that was installed was not the carpet that was purchased. It wasn't even the same color of "tan."

> **NCPHIF TIP:** Ask to see all invoices, paperwork, and warranties for all materials used so that you can confirm that you are getting exactly what you paid for.

SCAM ALERT!

THE VICTIM: A homeowner who hires a contractor who insists he can do it all.

THE SCAM: A homeowner happened to mention to his plumber that he wanted to have a wheelchair ramp installed for his disabled sister. The plumber told the homeowner he could do it for less than anyone else. Since the plumber did a great job on the bathroom sink and installed the toilet perfectly, the homeowner hired him to put on the ramp. The plumber did not bother to get a permit for the ramp and knew nothing about weight distribution. When the sister used the ramp for the first time, part of the ramp collapsed. The homeowner called the plumber but he never returned his calls.

> **NCPHIF TIP:** Be sure to ask the contractor what he specializes in. It might be a good idea to ask him what he specializes in before you tell him what you need done.

These are just some of the scams we are aware of. If you know of any other scams, contact us at **www.PreventContractorFraud. org** and let us know. Thank you for helping us protect others!

Conclusion

We hope that we have been able to provide you with valuable information to help you manage your project with your contractor. Most of all, we hope that the process goes smoothly and you now have a contractor who you can trust and rely on.

We want to hear from you! Visit us at **www.PreventContractor Fraud.org** and tell us:

- If you have a question
- How your project went
- If you had any problems
- If you were scammed
- If you have some advice to give

We would appreciate your feedback on what you thought about this book. Please email your comments to **book@ncphif.org**.

If you appreciate the hard work we are doing and would like to help us help others, please visit our website at **www. PreventContractorFraud.org** for ways to support our mission.

We would be honored if you would "like" us on Facebook and "follow" us on Twitter! Please visit our website for more information on our nonprofit organization:

www.PreventContractorFraud.org

Index

www.ingramcontent.com/pod-product-compliance
Lightning Source LLC
LaVergne TN
LVHW051514080426
835509LV00017B/2061